The
Mind Map®
Book

Ron Arns

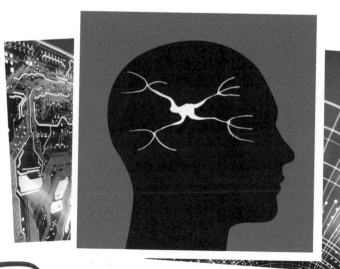

BBC

The
Mind Map®
Book

Unlock your creativity, boost your memory, change your life

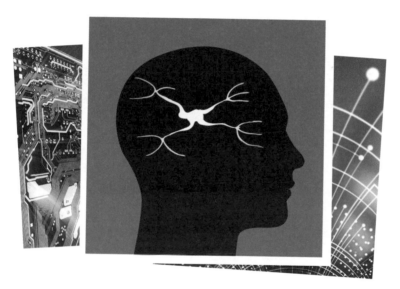

Tony Buzan™
and Barry Buzan

with James Harrison, consultant editor

Harlow, England • London • New York • Boston • San Francisco • Toronto • Sydney • Singapore • Hong Kong
Tokyo • Seoul • Taipei • New Delhi • Cape Town • Madrid • Mexico City • Amsterdam • Munich • Paris • Milan

Published by BBC Active, an imprint of Educational Publishers LLP, part of the Pearson Education Group, Edinburgh Gate, Harlow, Essex CM20 2JE, England.

First published in Great Britain in 2010

BBC logo © BBC 1996. BBC and BBC ACTIVE are trademarks of the British Broadcasting Corporation.

The right of Tony Buzan to be identified as author of this work has been asserted by him in accordance with the Copyright, Designs and Patents Act 1988.

ISBN: 978-1-4066-4716-7

British Library Cataloguing-in-Publication Data
A catalogue record for this book is available from the British Library

Library of Congress Cataloging-in-Publication Data
A catalog record for this book is available from the Library of Congress

10 9 8 7 6 5
13 12 11

Designed by Design Deluxe
Illustrations by Bill Piggins (unless otherwise stated)
Typeset in 9.5 Swis721 Lt BT by 30
Printed and bound in Great Britain by Ashford Colour Press Ltd, Gosport, Hampshire

The publisher's policy is to use paper manufactured from sustainable forests.

We dedicate this book

to all those Warriors of the Mind fighting,

in the Age of Intelligence,

the Century of the Brain

and Millennium of the Mind,

for the expansion

and freedom of Human Intelligence.

Contents

Part 4 Mind Maps in study, life and work 117

Part 5 Mind Maps and the future 169

Author's acknowledgements

We would like to express once again our great appreciation and enormous thanks to: our parents, Gordon and Jean Buzan, for launching us on this incredible journey, and especially to Mum for the depth of caring and days of work she contributed to the preparation of the original manuscript; Lorraine Gill, the artist, for her profound insights into the importance and nature of seeing, the image and the relationship of art to the brain, memory and creativity; Deborah Buzan for sustained encouragement and support over the many years of this project; Michael J. Gelb for his persistent and impassioned support of us, this book and a mind mapping world; our friends who spent so much time both reading and helping us with the various drafts – Lynn and the late Paul Collins, who among many other things helped us realise that a quantum leap was a small one!; Judy Caldwell, who was able to criticise in the true sense of the word, firing us with enthusiasm as she did so; John Humble, whose support for the concept of Mind Mapping over the years has provided a constant emotional strength; Sean Adam, for his enormous personal support, his 35-year commitment to the project and his consistent friendly cajoling of Tony to 'get that book out'; George Hughes, the first to apply successfully the Mind Map Family Study Technique; Edward Hughes, who applied Radiant Thinking and Mind Mapping to 'ace' Cambridge University; Dr Andrew Strigner, for helping to keep the radiant mind radiating; Peter Russell, the *Brain Book* man, for his continuing support; Geraldine Schwartz, who has done so much to help nurture the concept; Caro, Peter, Doris, Tanya and Julian Ayre for providing support, sustenance, and the beautiful home and grounds of Greenham Hall, where much of the first edition was written; the Folley Family, for providing a home and work area of exquisite quality.

Bringing *The Mind Map Book* into the twenty-first century, 'the Century of the Brain', has been a global team effort, and I would like to extend my heartfelt appreciation to the entire network of Buzan Centres International, now well and truly established – and growing! Thank you to all the Buzan Master Trainers and Licensed Instructors from Buzan World for your Mind Maps and case studies and much valued contributions, especially Masanori Kanda, Mikiko Chikada Kawase, Ken Ito and Shiro Kobayashi in Japan, and to Henry Toi and Eric Cheung in Singapore. I would also like to extend a special acknowledgement to Henry and Eric as well as to Thum Cheng Cheong and the Buzan Asia team who created the brilliant *Dream! – The Amazing Journey of Putting Singapore on the Map*, dealing with the story of creating the biggest

Mind Map in the world, which has been adapted for this new edition. Thank you also to Po Chung in Hong Kong for his invaluable Mind Map contribution, to Tanya Phonanan, founder, Buzan Centers, in Thailand for his Mind Map and story and to Jorge O. Castañeda, President, Buzan Latin America, whose pioneering work is transforming educational, business and government thinking throughout Latin America. Greetings and thanks also to Bill Jarrard and Jennifer Goddard at Buzan Centre Australia/NZ for their unceasing creative efforts in bringing Mind Maps to the world. In Europe I would like to thank Hilde Jaspaert for her excellently drawn Mind Maps and her creative mind mapping input to the book, as well as on the Buzan Mind Map seminar circuit. Hilde can be contacted at **www.inter-activeminds.com**.

Back in the UK I must thank first and foremost Chris Griffiths, Chief Executive Buzan Online Ltd, for his expert input for the computer mind mapping chapter and his brilliant development of iMindMap, now in Version 4.0. Fantastic visual and text support was also provided by Emily Van Keogh and the team based at Buzan Online in Cardiff including Melina Costi and Owen Hardy.

Thank you also to Raymond Keene OBE, Chess Grandmaster and Mind Sports Correspondent for *The Times*, for his indefatigable steer and support; and to Brian Lee for being a friend and stalwart in helping me to bring Mind Maps to the business and educational worlds, to Phil Chambers, World Mind Mapping Champion and Senior Buzan Licensed Instructor, for his superb Mind Map creations and for his tireless backroom input!

Without my 'home team' at Buzan HQ this book would have been a logistical nightmare: therefore a heartfelt thank you must go to Pauline Aleski, Anne Reynolds, Suzi Rockett, and Jenny Redman for superb logistical support and effort.

At Pearson, the publishers, I would like to thank Richard Stagg, Director, who was a prime figure in the launching of this project; and to add my profound thanks to Samantha Jackson, my cherished Commissioning Editor, for her total commitment to Mind Maps and to this book throughout its long gestation; also to her team in Harlow: Caroline Jordan, Gillian Wallis, Laura Blake. My thanks would not be complete without acknowledgement to James Harrison, my independent Consultant Editor and supreme juggler, for taking on the seemingly impossible task of pulling everything together.

Finally my acknowledgements to all those mind mapping business people and educators who have enthusiastically provided Mind Maps and stories, both for the first edition and this revised and updated edition, and who for reasons of space I have either omitted to thank or been unable to include.

Dear reader, a special thanks to you for joining the growing global community of Mind Map practitioners in business. *Please* do contact me with your business and work-related Mind Maps and stories for possible inclusion in the next edition of *The Mind Map Book* **tony.buzan@buzanworld.com**.

Publisher's acknowledgements

We are grateful to the following for permission to reproduce copyright material:
P. Sole, ISM/Science Photo Library, page 6; David Mack/ Science Photo Library, page 7; Syndics of Cambridge University Library, page 14; The Royal Collection © 2009 Her Majesty Queen Elizabeth II, page 15; Julian Baum/Science Photo Library, page 24; Martin Ruegner/photolibrary, page 25; Rachel Warne/Science Photo Library, page 35; William Gray/photolibrary, page 47; Royal Observatory, Edinburgh/AAO/Science Photo Library, page 191.

For technical reasons all but five of the Mind Maps in this book have been copied (these are named in the following list as 'original'). All other artworks detailed below have been redrawn by Julian Bingley. The Mind Maps, however, remain the copyright of their owners as listed below.

Sean Adam, page 112; Tony Bigonia, Richard Kohler, Matthew Puk, John Ragsdale, Chris Slabach, Thomas Spinola, Thomas Sullivan, Lorita Williams, page 153; Claudius Borer (original), page 78; Tony Buzan, page 132 (original), page 138 (original), page 145 (original), page 160 (top); Kathy De Stefano, page 79 (top); Ulf Ekberg (original), page 82; Thomas Enskog, page 142; Dr John Geesink, page 79 (bottom); Lorraine Gill, page 33; Sheikh Hamad, page 198; Hilde Jaspaert, page 90; Mikiko Chikada Kawase, page 125; Raymond Keene OBE, page 160 (bottom); James Lee, page 143; Katarina Naiman, page 141 (bottom); Karen Schmidt, page 141 (top); Lars Soderberg, page 193; C.C. Thum, page 81; Benjamin Zander, page 98. The authors of the Mind Maps on pages 123 and 124 prefer not to be named.

Every effort has been made by the publisher to obtain permission from the appropriate source to reproduce material which appears in this book. In some instances we may have been unable to trace the owners of copyright material and would appreciate any information that would enable us to do so.

Foreword

The physicist Niels Bohr once admonished a student, 'You're not thinking, you're just being logical.' So I'd like to think that logic is not the criteria by which we evaluate our potential. The brain is actually very different from a 'logical' computer.

In the twenty-first century it is more important than ever to understand the brain. We are all living longer and healthier lives, but we sometimes forget that there is no point in living longer and healthier lives if we don't keep the brain healthy too. A healthy brain means ensuring we keep the brain active – using our memories, thinking effectively and being creative – ultimately to reach our individual potentials which, not so long ago, was circumscribed by birth and by health; we simply lived out a certain destiny.

Now we are in a position to ask the big questions: 'What am I doing with my life?' 'What is it all about?' And I think brain research is 'coming of age' not just by asking how to make people better or even how to have a better memory – though these are highly welcome developments – but also tackling the most exciting questions of 'What makes me the individual I am?' and 'How can I stretch my potential?'

I applaud Tony for celebrating the brain, especially the brain in the twenty-first century – something he has been at the forefront of for over 40 years – and really the mind, and I recommend his highly stimulating *Mind Set* series (*The Mind Map Book*, *The Memory Book*, *The Speed Reading Book* and *Use Your Head*) of brain improvement books – your adventure is just beginning.

Baroness Professor Susan Greenfield, CBE
Director of the Royal Institution of Great Britain, Fullerian Professor
of Psychology, Honorary Fellow, Senior Research Fellow and
Holder of the Ordre National de la Legion d'Honneur

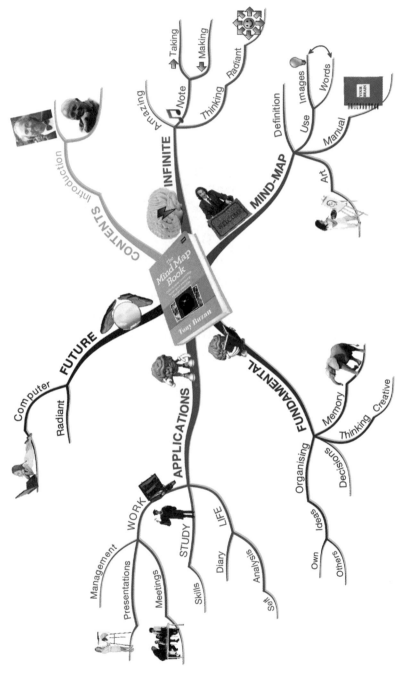

A Mind Map overview of the entire book you are about to read

Introduction

Tony Buzan

Since my invention of Mind Maps during the 1960s, they have become known as the 'ultimate thinking tool'. They have taken me on a fascinating journey that has transformed my life, and I hope *The Mind Map Book* will help you transform yours for the better too.

As a direct result of Mind Maps, the 14th International Conference on Thinking held at University Putra Malaysia, Kuala Lumpur, in 2009, in conjunction with Malaysia's Higher Education Minister Datuk Seri Mohamed Khaled Nordin, officially declared the twenty-first century to be the Century of the Brain, and the current millennium to be the Millennium of the Mind. The Minister also formally declared that we have moved through the Ages of Agriculture, Industry, Information and Knowledge into the new Age of Intelligence – and the Mind Map is the 'ultimate thinking tool' for intelligence.

In its relatively short life, the Mind Map has generated over 200 million pages of reference; it has been seen on television by over a billion people and has reached nearly half the population of the planet through radio and the press.

As you read *The Mind Map Book*, you will be joining a global revolution in thinking that is already transforming the way we think about our mind's potential and the way we use our brains and our multiple intelligences. Here's how it all began.

In my second year at university, I strode purposefully into the library, and asked the librarian where I could find a book on my brain and how to use it. She immediately directed me to the medical section of the library. When I explained that I did not wish to *operate* on my brain, but to *use* it, I was politely informed that there were no such books. I left the library in astonishment.

Like others around me, I was going through the typical student's 'pilgrim's progress': the slow realisation that the volume of academic work is increasing and that the brain is starting to buckle under the strain of all the thinking, reading, creativity, memory, problem-solving, analysis and writing required. Again, like others, I had begun to experience not only diminishing returns but accelerating *non-returns*. The more I took notes and studied, the less, paradoxically, I seemed to succeed!

The logical progression of either situation led me to catastrophe. If I cut down my studying, I would not absorb the necessary information and would consequently do progressively badly; if I were studying harder, making more notes, putting in more time, I was similarly spiralling into failure. The answer,

I assumed, must lie in the way I was using my intelligence and thinking skills – hence my visit to the library.

As I walked away from the library that day, I realised that the 'problem' of not being able to find the books I needed was actually a blessing in disguise. For if such books were not available, then I had happened upon virgin territory of the most staggering importance.

I began to study every area of knowledge I felt would help shed light on the basic questions:

- How do I learn how to learn?
- What is the nature of my thinking?
- What are the best techniques for memorising?
- What are the best techniques for creative thinking?
- What are the best current techniques for faster and efficient reading?
- What are the best current techniques for thinking in general?
- Is there a possibility of developing new thinking techniques or one master technique?

As a consequence of these questions, I began to study psychology, the neuro-physiology of the brain, semantics, neuro-linguistics, information theory, memory and mnemonic techniques, perception, creative thinking, the notes of the great thinkers in all disciplines and the general sciences. Gradually I realised that the human brain functioned more effectively and efficiently if its various physical aspects and intellectual skills were allowed to work harmoniously with each other, rather than being divided.

The tiniest things produced the most significant and satisfying results. For example, simply combining two skills – words and colours – that exist in different hemispheres of the brain transformed my note-taking. The simple addition of two colours to my notes improved my memory of those notes significantly, and, perhaps even more importantly, made me begin to *enjoy* what I was doing.

Little by little, an overall architecture began to emerge, and as it did, I began to coach, as a hobby, pupils who had been described as 'learning disabled', 'hopeless', 'dyslexic', 'attention disorder', 'backward' and 'delinquent'. All these so-called 'failures' very rapidly changed into good students, a number of them rising to the top of their respective classes.

One young girl, Barbara, had been told that she had the lowest IQ her school had ever registered. Within a month of learning how to learn, she raised her IQ to 160, and eventually graduated as the top student from her college. Pat, a young American of extraordinary talent, who had been falsely categorised as learning disabled, subsequently said (after having shattered a number of creativity and memory tests), 'I wasn't learning *disabled*; I was learning *deprived*.'

By the early 1970s artificial intelligence had arrived and I could buy a megabyte computer and with that computer I could receive a 1,000-page operating manual. Yet, in our supposedly advanced stage of civilisation – the Age, at that time, of Information – we were all coming into the world with the most astoundingly complex super-computer, *quadrillions* of times more powerful than any known computer, and where were *our* operating manuals?!

It was then that I decided to write a series of books based on my research: *An Encyclopedia of the Brain and Its Use*. I started in 1971, and as I did so the image on the horizon became ever clearer – it was the growing concept of Radiant Thinking, Mind Mapping and a mentally literate world. With the publication of this latest edition of *The Mind Map Book*, with the blossoming amount of research on mind mapping now being done around the world, and with the number of users now topping an estimated 500 million, the vision speeds ever closer to fruition.

Throughout the 1970s, 80s and 90s, I travelled the world lecturing to governments, businesses, universities and schools about my 'new baby' and writing the first edition of *The Mind Map Book*, which eventually appeared in 1995.

One of my dreams has been to develop the Mind Map software that could create Mind Maps on screen in the same way they are generated by the human brain. The task was far more difficult than I had originally envisaged, and it was not until the spring of 2009 with the launch of iMindMap Version 4.0 that the first *real* Mind Mapping software appeared – thanks to the work of the computer Mind Mapping genius Chris Griffiths and his incredible team. This new edition of *The Mind Map Book* will introduce you, for the first time, to the interlinking of the human brain to the computer brain, and show how each 'intelligence' improves the functioning of the other.

In the early stages of developing the Mind Map, I envisaged mind mapping being used primarily for memory. However, after months of discussion, my brother Barry convinced me that creative thinking was an equally important application of this technique.

Barry had been working on the theory of mind mapping from a very different perspective, and his contribution enormously accelerated my development of the mind mapping process. Here is his own story.

Barry Buzan

I dovetailed with Tony's idea of Mind Maps in 1970, shortly after I had settled in London. At that time, the idea was only just beginning to take on an identity of its own, but was showing its potential to be as distinct from mere key word note-taking as could be previously imagined. It was just one part of Tony's broader agenda of learning methods and understanding of the human brain. As a sometime participant in Tony's work, I was on the fringes of this developmental process. My own serious engagement with the technique began when I started to apply it to the business of writing a doctoral thesis.

What attracted me about mind mapping was not the note-*taking* application that had captivated Tony, but the note-*making* one. I needed not only to organise a growing mass of research data, but also to clarify my thoughts on my thesis of the convoluted political question of why peace movements almost always fail to achieve their stated objectives. My experience was that Mind Maps were a more powerful tool for thinking because they enabled me to sketch out the main ideas and to see quickly and clearly how they related to each other. They provided me with an exceptionally useful intermediate stage between the thinking process and actually committing words to paper.

I soon realised that the problem of bridging the gap between thinking and writing was a major deciding factor in success or failure for my fellow postgraduate students. Many failed to bridge this gap. They became more and more knowledgeable about their research subject but less and less able to pull all the details together in order to write about it.

Mind mapping gave me a tremendous competitive advantage. It enabled me to assemble and refine my ideas without going through the time-consuming process of drafting and re-drafting. By separating thinking from writing, I was able to think more clearly and extensively. When it was time to start writing, I already had a clear structure and a firm sense of direction, and this made the writing easier, faster and more enjoyable. I completed my doctorate in under the prescribed three years, and also had time to write a chapter for another book, help to found, and then edit, a new quarterly journal of international relations, be associate editor of the student newspaper, take up motorcycling and get married (doing a Mind Map with my wife-to-be to compose our wedding vows). Because of these experiences, my enthusiasm for the creative thinking side of the technique grew.

Mind mapping remains a central element in my whole approach to academic work. It has made it possible for me to sustain an unusually high output of books, articles and conference papers. It has helped me to remain a generalist in a field where the weight of information forces most people to become specialists. I also credit it with enabling me to write clearly about theoretical matters whose complexity all too often inspires incomprehensible prose. Its impact on my career is perhaps best reflected in the surprise with which I am frequently greeted when first meeting people: 'You are much younger than I expected. How could you have written so much in such a short time?'

Having experienced the dramatic effect of Mind Maps on my own life and work, I became a propagandist for the particular importance of creative thinking within the broader range of applications that Tony was developing.

At the end of the 1970s, Tony decided that there should be a book about mind mapping, and we discussed how I might participate in this project. In the intervening decades we had developed very different styles. From his teaching and writing work, Tony had worked out a very wide range of applications, had begun to link the technique to brain theory and had worked out many of the rules of form. As an academic writer, I had ploughed a much narrower furrow. My Mind Maps incorporated only a few elements of form, almost no colour or image, and evolved a rather different basic architecture. I used them almost exclusively for writing projects, though I increasingly, and with great benefit, took them up for lecturing and management tasks. I learned how to think deeply over long periods, using Mind Maps to structure and sustain large research projects.

There were several reasons why we wanted to collaborate on this book. One was the thought that by synthesising our two understandings, we would produce a better book. Another was that we shared a profound enthusiasm for Mind Maps, and wanted to make them more widely available to the world. A third reason was the frustration I had experienced when trying to teach some of my students the technology of mind mapping. Several unsuccessful attempts convinced me that Tony was right when he said that people needed to be taught not just a technique but also how to think. I wanted a book that I could give to people and say: 'This will teach you how to think and work as I do.'

The working process that ensued has been very long. It has taken the form of a sustained dialogue at regular but infrequent intervals, in which each of us has tried to bring the other to a full understanding of his own ideas. About 80 per cent of the book is Tony's: all the brain theory, the linkage of creativity and memory, the rules, much of the technique, nearly all the stories and all the linkage to other research. His also is the prose, for he did nearly all the drafting. My main contributions were in the structuring of the book, and the argument that the real power of Mind Maps is unleashed through the use of basic ordering ideas (the 'chapter headings' or key concepts – that is, the first-level branches of the Mind Map). Beyond that, I played the role of critic, foil, nag, support and co-idea-generator.

It took a long time before we fully understood and appreciated each other's insights, but eventually we reached an almost complete consensus. Although slow, joint writing can sometimes produce a book that has much more range and depth than either author could have achieved alone. This is such a work.

Tony Buzan

As Barry has stated, we have practised what we preached, and preached what we practised, in that we have used the Mind Map itself to write *The Mind Map Book*. Over a period of 15 years, we have composed individual brainstorming Mind Maps, and then met and interlinked our two sets of ideas. After deep discussion, we have incubated and blended the next set of ideas, spent time observing natural phenomena, individually mind mapped our conceptions of the next stage, and once again met in order to compare and move on. The Mind Map of the complete book generated the individual Mind Maps for the chapters, each Mind Map forming the basis for the text of that chapter.

The process has given new meaning to the word 'brother', and especially to the word 'brotherhood'. Even as we were writing about it, we realised that we ourselves had created a 'group Mind Map' that contained all the elements of our individual minds as well as the explosively synergetic results of their meeting.

Today, many years from when the first edition of *The Mind Map Book* was published, 'mind mapping' has become a phrase familiar to many, and, indeed it has become a global phenomenon. But the potential it possesses to revolutionise the way we think is something you, the reader, may not be aware of. We certainly realise there is still plenty of work to be done in harnessing the Mind Map to manage 'the manager of knowledge'– that is, the brain – in education, in the workplace and in our work–life balance. And that is why I continue unceasingly to tour the globe to showcase 'Mind Maps, Memory and Creativity' in my lectures, seminars and workshops. It is also the spur to promote the 'Festival of The Mind' and its umbrella activities, including the World Memory Championships (with my friend and colleague International Chess Grandmaster Raymond Keene OBE), and other Buzan online activities listed in the online resources section at the end of the book.

As technology has evolved, mind mapping software has been developed, culminating in the launch of iMindMap – my official Mind Map software. This has led to a rise in popularity within business and education and personal use, as people utilise mind mapping software to help them organise, plan and think creatively. As one of the world's best-known entrepreneurs Bill Gates sees it, the 'new generation of mind mapping software can [also] be used as a digital "blank slate" to help connect and synthesize ideas and data – and ultimately create new knowledge'.

We sincerely hope that *The Mind Map Book* gives you the same thrill of discovery, excitement in exploration and sheer delight in the creative generation of ideas and communication that we have ourselves experienced.

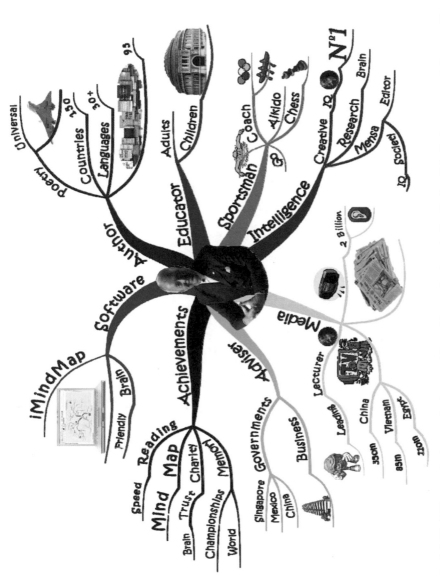

A classic example of a full Mind Map employing words, images, hierarchies and categorisation that radiate their own associations and increase the power of memory. It is a Mind Map about the author Tony Buzan

The **human brain** is an enchanted loom where millions of **flashing shuttles** weave a dissolving pattern, always a **meaningful pattern**, though never an abiding one, a shifting harmony of **sub-patterns**. It is as if the Milky Way entered upon some **cosmic dance**.

Sir Charles Sherrington

Part 1
The infinite power and potential of your mind

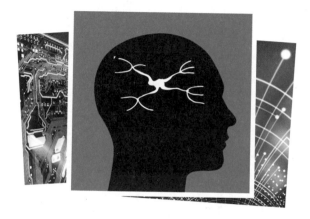

Only during the last few centuries have we begun gathering information about the structure and workings of our brains. Although still a very long way from a complete understanding (we are increasingly aware that what we do know is only a tiny fraction of what there is to be known), we now know enough to change, for ever, our view of others and ourselves.

Part 1 introduces you to the amazing natural make-up of your brain and to the astonishing way the mind works. You will find out how the universally regarded geniuses used skills that are available to everyone, and why it is that 95 per cent of people are dissatisfied with their mental functioning. This part ends with a new, brain-based mode of advanced thought: Radiant Thinking, which in turn leads us naturally on to the Mind Map.

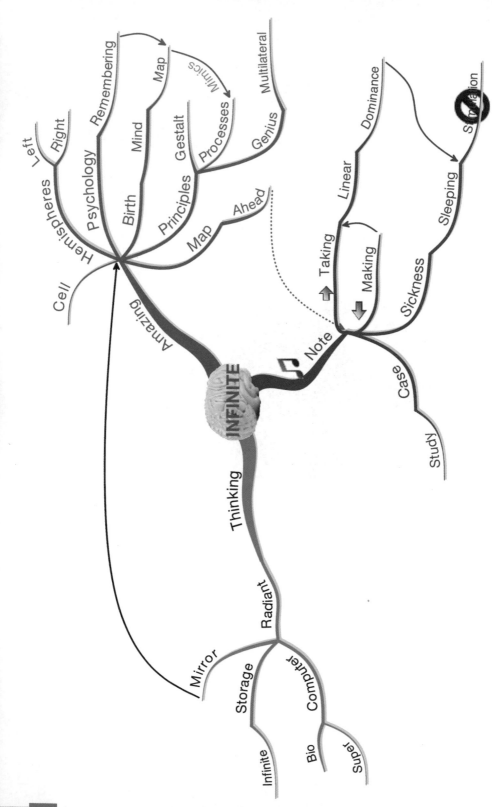

A breakdown in Mind Map form of the first three chapters of The Mind Map Book

The infinite power and potential of your mind

Your amazing brain

This chapter reveals the extraordinary functions of the human brain. You will discover how many brain cells you have and how they interact in astoundingly complex and sophisticated ways. You will also discover the true nature of your brain's information-processing systems; and how the left and right hemispheres are in constant communication while performing different functions. As you read about the nature and workings of your brain, you will realise its startling capacity and power.

Modern brain research

The brain cell

We now know it isn't just millions, but an estimated one million million brain cells that reside in each human brain. The brain cells that do the thinking (called neurons) make up one hundred billion cells. Each one contains a vast electrochemical complex and a powerful micro-data-processing and transmitting system that, despite its complexity, would fit on the head of a pin. Each of these brain cells looks like a super-octopus, with a central body and tens, hundreds or thousands of tentacles.

As we increase the level of magnification, we see that the tentacles are like the fine branches of a tree, radiating from the cell centre or nucleus. The branches of the brain cell are called dendrites (defined as 'natural tree-like markings or structures'). One particularly large and long branch, called the axon, is the main exit for information transmitted by that cell. Each dendrite and axon may range from 1 millimetre to 1.5 metres in length, and all along and around its length are little mushroom-like protuberances called dendritic spines and synaptic buttons.

Moving further into this super-microscopic world, we find that each dendritic spine/synaptic button contains bundles of chemicals which are the major message-carriers in our human thinking process. A dendritic spine/synaptic button from one brain cell will link with a synaptic button from another brain cell. When an electrical impulse travels through the brain cell, chemicals will be transferred across the minute, liquid-filled space between the two. (It is important to realise that the neurons are not joined to each other.) This space is called the synaptic gap. The chemicals 'slot into' the receiving surface, creating an impulse that travels through the receiving brain cell from where it is directed to an adjoining brain cell.

A brain cell may receive incoming pulses from hundreds of thousands of connecting points every second. Acting like a vast telephone exchange, the cell will instantaneously compute, nanosecond by nanosecond, the sum data of all incoming information, and will redirect it along the appropriate path.

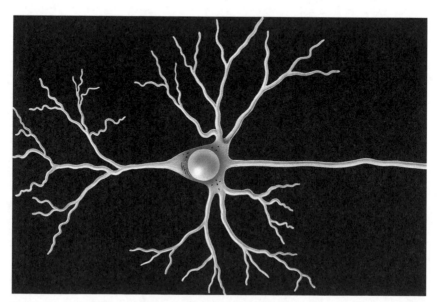

Multipolar neuron (nerve cell) reflecting Mind Map structure

The infinite power and potential of your mind

Forming mental maps

As a given message, or thought, or relived memory is passed from brain cell to brain cell, a biochemical electromagnetic pathway is established. Each of these neuronal pathways is known as a 'memory trace'. These memory traces or mental maps are one of the most exciting areas of modern brain research and have brought us to some startling conclusions.

Every time you have a thought, the biochemical/electromagnetic resistance along the pathway carrying that thought is reduced. It is like trying to clear a path through a forest. The first time is a struggle because you have to fight your way through the undergrowth. The second time you travel that way will be easier because of the clearing you did on your first journey. The more times you travel that path, the less resistance there will be, until, after many repetitions, you have a wide, smooth track which requires little or no clearing. A similar function occurs in your brain: the more you repeat patterns or maps of thought, the less resistance there is to them. Therefore, and of greater significance, repetition in itself increases the probability of repetition. In other words, the more times a 'mental event' happens, the more likely it is to happen again.

Infinite possibilities

The results of a 60-year investigation into the nature of our brain cells led Professor Petr Kouzmich Anokhin of Moscow University to conclude in his paper 'The Forming of Natural and Artificial Intelligence' that:

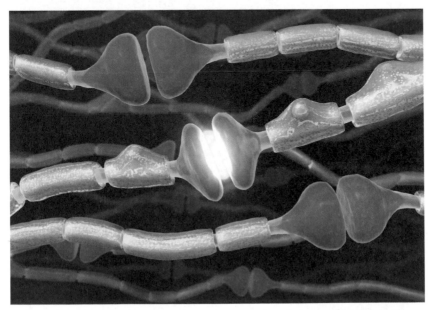

Image of synapses interconnecting between two brain cells transmitting information

We can show that each of the ten billion neurons in the human brain has a possibility of connections of one with twenty-eight noughts after it! If a single neuron has this quality of potential, we can hardly imagine what the whole brain can do. What it means is that the total number of possible combinations/permutations in the brain, if written out, would be 1 followed by 10.5 million kilometres of noughts! No human yet exists who can use all the potential of his brain. This is why we don't accept any pessimistic estimates of the limits of the human brain. It is unlimited!

Each individual brain cell is capable of contacting and embracing as many as 10,000 or more proximate brain cells in the same instant. It is in these embraces that the infinite patterns, the infinite 'maps of your mind', are created, nurtured and grown.

Your brain's left and right sides

In the late 1960s, Professor Roger Sperry of California, who was subsequently awarded the Nobel Prize for his research, announced the results of his investigation into the brain's most highly evolved area, the cerebral cortex ('cortex' meaning 'outer shell' or bark).

Sperry's initial findings indicated that the two sides, or hemispheres, of the cortex tend to divide the major intellectual functions between them. The right hemisphere appeared to be dominant in the following intellectual areas: rhythm, spatial awareness, gestalt (wholeness), imagination, daydreaming, colour and dimension. The left hemisphere appeared dominant in a different but equally powerful range of mental skills: words, logic, numbers, sequence, linearity, analysis and lists.

It was also found out that, although each hemisphere is dominant in certain activities, they are both basically skilled in *all* areas, and the mental skills identified by Roger Sperry are actually distributed *throughout* the cortex.

We often say people are either left-side (scientists) or right-side (artists) dominant, but saying this limits our potential – we can be, and fundamentally are, both. As cognitive neuropsychologist Michael Bloch concluded, 'if we call ourselves "right brain" or "left brain" people, we are limiting our ability to develop new strategies'.

The main intellectual functions of the two sides of the brain

The psychology of learning – remembering

Research has shown that, during the learning process, the human brain primarily remembers the following:

- Items from the beginning of the learning period ('the primacy effect').

- Items from the end of the learning period ('the recency effect').

- Any items associated with things or patterns already stored, or linked to other aspects of what is being learned.

- Any items which are emphasised as being in some way outstanding or unique.

- Any items which appeal particularly strongly to any of the five senses.

- Those items which are of particular interest to the person.

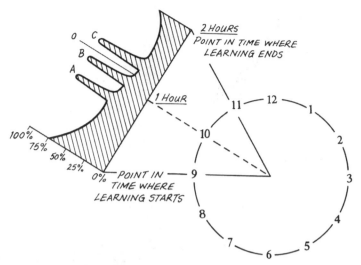

Figure 1.1 Graph predicting the high and low points of recall during a learning period. The reasons for the high points can be used to construct the basis for a new theory of learning

The list of findings taken together with the graph shown above gives you information that is of critical importance in understanding the way your brain works.

The birth of the Mind Map

It was by virtue of exploring how memory and understanding do not work in the same way (and not the 'left–right brain theory', as many have assumed) which gave rise to my development of the Mind Map. In the 1960s, while lecturing at various universities on the psychology of learning and memory, I began to notice the enormous discrepancy between the theory I was teaching and what I was actually doing.

My lecture notes were standard linear notes, providing an inherent amount of forgetting and inbuilt amount of non-communication. I was using the notes as the basis of lectures on memory in which I was pointing out that two of the main factors in recall were association and emphasis. Yet these elements were singularly lacking in my own notes! By constantly asking myself the question, 'What, in my notes, will help me to associate and emphasise?' I arrived, by the start of the 1960s, at an embryonic concept of the Mind Map.

My subsequent investigations into the nature of information processing, the structure and functioning of the brain cell, research into the cerebral cortex and the note-taking habits of geniuses confirmed and buttressed the original theory, and Mind Maps were born.

The infinite power and potential of your mind

Gestalt – the 'completing tendency'

Our brains tend to look for pattern and completion. For instance, most people, reading the words 'One, two, three . . .' will have to fight the impulse to add 'four'. Similarly, if someone says, 'I have the most fascinating story to tell you . . . Oops! Sorry, I've just realised I'm not supposed to tell anyone,' your mind will scream for completion! This inbuilt tendency of the brain to search for completion is also known as gestalt – the natural 'completing tendency' to fill in the blank spaces with new words and images. And it is this gestalt that is satisfied by the structure of the Mind Map. The Mind Map allows an infinite sequence of associative 'probes' which comprehensively investigate any idea or question with which you are concerned.

Thought processes of the brain

This amazing machine, your brain, has five major thought-processing functions – receiving, holding, analysing, outputting and controlling:

Receiving: Anything taken in by any of your senses.

Holding: Your memory, including retention (the ability to store information) and recall (the ability to access that stored information).

Analysing: Pattern-recognition and information-processing.

Outputting: Any form of communication or creative act, including thinking.

Controlling: Referring to all mental and physical functions.

These five categories all reinforce each other:

1 It's easier to **receive** data if you are interested and motivated, and if the receiving process is compatible with brain functions.

2 Having **received** the information efficiently, you will find it easier to **hold** and **analyse** it. Conversely, efficient **holding** and **analysis** will increase your ability to receive information. Similarly, **analysis**, which involves a complex array of information-processing tasks, requires an ability to **hold** (retain and associate) the data which has been received.

3 The quality of the **analysis** will obviously be affected by your ability to **receive** and **hold** the information.

4 These three functions converge into the fourth – the outputting or expression by Mind Map, speech, gesture and so on of that which has been **received**, **held** and **analysed**.

5 The fifth category, **controlling**, refers to your brain's general monitoring of all your mental and physical functions, including general health, attitude and environmental conditions. This category is particularly important because a healthy mind and a healthy body are essential if the other four functions of **receiving**, **holding**, **analysing** and **outputting** are to operate at their full potential.

The Mind Map mimics thought processes

Creating a Mind Map requires 'whole-brain', synergetic thinking that reflects the explosive nature of the neurons zapping across the brain in search of new connections during the process of thinking. It is like some vast pinball machine with billions of silver balls whizzing at the speed of light from flipper to flipper.

Your brain does *not* think linearly or sequentially like a computer. It thinks *multilaterally*: radiantly. When you create a Mind Map, the branches grow outwards to form another level of sub-branches encouraging you to create ever more ideas out of each thought you add – just as your brain does. Also, because all the ideas on the Mind Map are linked to each other, it helps your brain, through association, to make great leaps of understanding and imagination.

Geniuses think multilaterally

All the great visionaries were able to visualise and to create a powerful internal vision of their goals and ambitions almost to the exclusion of everything else; constructive daydreaming enabled Einstein to 'see' how the universe was shaped. The geniuses incorporated imagination in the form of images in their notes.

Unlike many of their contemporaries, they understood how to tap into the power of their brains and use their resources. Below we've created a list of these mental skills for you to analyse – and copy! As you'll see, the skills can be learnt by anyone, and once you understand how to mind map and release your capacity to think, remember and create, you too could be a genius!

- *Vision*: The 'guiding light' in having a clear goal of succeeding in your life's ambition. Muhammad Ali's vision of victory was so complete he would often predict how his next fight would pan out.

- *Desire*: The degree of passion or wish to accomplish your vision, goals and mission. That passion can often be 'burning', as with Faraday's desire to explore the world of electricity even though he was a bookbinder by trade.

- *Planning*: This involves clarity of focus for accomplishing the overall vision. Qin Shi Huangdi, the first Ch'in Emperor, encapsulated this with his reorganisation of China, including the building of the Great Wall of China.

- *Subject knowledge*: The great geniuses acquired a vast and fundamental knowledge-base in the fields they wished to pursue.

- *Mental literacy*: Understanding the brain's behavioural skills, especially memory, creativity, learning and general thinking skills.

The great brains

One other attribute the great geniuses shared was constant note-taking – Edison alone has around 5 million pages or more relating to his 60-year career as an inventor, developer, manufacturer, entrepreneur and judicious businessman. For those of you who have been criticised for making 'messy notes' or 'doodling', what follows will provide consolation and vindication!

During my lectures over the past 35 years I have frequently displayed the notes of an unidentified thinker generally recognised as 'great'. I have then invited course participants to identify the originator of the notes. In every group, the participants have mentioned – usually guessing wrongly – the names of da Vinci, Einstein, Picasso, Darwin, and at least one other major musician, scientist or politician. This experiment shows that we assume that people like da Vinci and Einstein must have achieved their greatness by using a wider range of mental skills than their peers. The two examples shown here of da Vinci and Darwin support this assumption, providing evidence that the Great Brains did indeed use more of their natural ability, and that – unlike their more linear-thinking contemporaries – they were intuitively beginning to use the principles of Radiant Thinking and Mind Mapping.

Using the full range of mental skills

A quick way of judging the excellence of your own or any set of notes is to look at the mental skills shown in the Mind Map on page 9 and check how many of these skills are incorporated in your notes – the more the better.

The notes in particular by Leonardo da Vinci demonstrate the point. He took copious notes which used words, symbols, sequence, listing, linearity, analysis, association, visual rhythm, numbers, imagery, dimension and gestalt – an example of a complete mind expressing itself completely. The notes by Charles Darwin, with their proto-Mind Map, are also an external expression of his thought processes.

We know that we could all utilise the same inherent mental power. So why are so many people now experiencing such massive problems with thinking, creativity, problem-solving, planning, memory, and dealing with change?

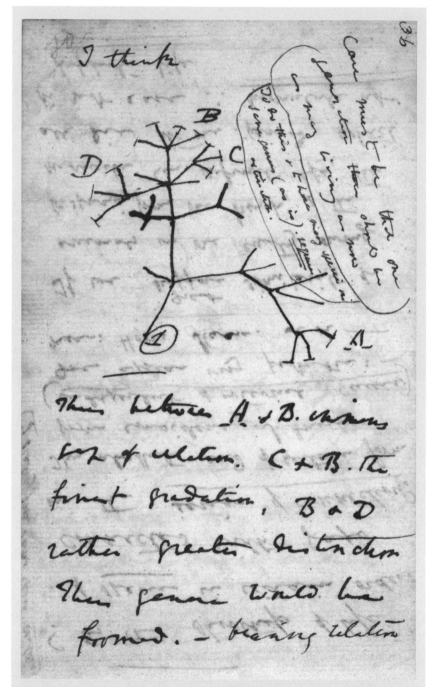

Charles Darwin's drawing of the tree of evolution follows the natural architecture of the Mind Map

The infinite power and potential of your mind

Leonardo da Vinci's notes utilise the full range of cortical skills

The road 'map' ahead

From the physiological and psychological evidence, we know that your brain contains vast power waiting to be unleashed. Our research on geniuses reveals that they used a greater proportion of their inherent mental power than those around them and, most importantly, we know we could *all* utilise the same inherent mental powers. So why aren't we? The next chapter explains why.

Note-making and note-taking

This chapter reveals the inherent weaknesses of note-making and note-taking systems currently used all over the world. By analysing the effectiveness (or ineffectiveness) of various styles of note-making and note-taking, we can begin to evolve a system that unlocks our natural creativity, thought processes, problem-solving and recall abilities.

The dominance of linear notes

We have researched the note-making and note-taking styles of individuals at all levels in schools, universities and various professions (note-making means organising your own thoughts, often creatively, and note-taking means summarising someone else's thoughts, as expressed in a book, article or lecture). This research has been carried out in many different countries and has included observation, questioning and practical experiments.

One of the experiments consisted of asking each member of the group to prepare, within five minutes, an innovative, creative speech on the topic 'The Brain, Innovation, Creativity and the Future'. They were allowed to use a wide variety of papers, coloured pens and other writing materials, and were asked to include the following 'triggers' in their notes: memory, decision-making, communication and presentation, time management, innovation and creativity, problem-solving, planning, humour, analysis and audience involvement.

Despite being offered a wide range of materials, the majority chose standard lined paper and a single (usually black, blue or grey) pen, and three major styles used in the experiment emerged:

- **The sentence/narrative style**: Writing out whatever is to be communicated in narrative form.

- **The list style**: Noting down the ideas as they occur.

- **The outline numerical/alphabetical style**: Making notes in a hierarchical sequence consisting of major categories and subcategories.

In every school, university and business we visited, the three major styles outlined above were used by more than 95 per cent of those tested. Many people combine various elements of these three major styles. All over the world, the current standard systems of note-making and note-taking are identical. While Middle Eastern and Asian notes may look different from Western notes, they actually use exactly the same elements. Although languages like Chinese, Japanese, Indian and Arabic are written vertically or right-to-left, rather than left-to-right, the presentation is still linear.

In each of the three major styles described, the main tools used were:

1 **Linear patterning**: The notes were usually written in straight lines. Grammar, chronological sequence and hierarchical sequence were also used.

2 **Symbols**: These included letters, words and numbers.

3 **Analysis**: This was used but its quality was adversely affected by the linear patterning, reflecting too great an emphasis on the linear nature of presentation rather than content.

Symbols, linear patterning, words, numbers and analysis form the major elements of current standard note-making and note-taking; but these are only a fraction of the many tools available to the cerebral cortex of the human brain.

Standard notes show an almost complete absence of:

- Visual rhythm

- Visual pattern or just pattern

- Colour

- Image (imagination)

- Visualisation

- Dimension

- Spatial awareness

- Gestalt (completing tendency)

- Association.

STYLE	PURPOSES	TOOLS
1	MEMORY	WORDS
	COMMUNICATION &	NUMBERS
	PRESENTATION	SEQUENCE
	INNOVATION &	LINES
2	CREATIVITY	LISTS
	PLANNING	LOGIC
	ANALYSIS	ANALYSIS
	DECISION MAKING	ONE-COLOUR
3	ETC	

The three major note-taking styles used by 95 per cent of note-takers and note-makers in all schools and professions around the world, regardless of language or nationality. Can you see why they leave 'brains in quandary'?

'Global Sleeping Sickness'

As these missing elements are essential in overall brain function, and specifically in recall during learning (as described on page 9), it is not surprising that most of those participating in our research found the whole business of taking notes frustrating and unproductive. Words most commonly associated with note-making and note-taking were: 'boring', 'punishment', 'headaches', 'wasted time' and 'failure'.

Over 95 per cent of the notes were written in a single colour, a monotone (usually blue, black or grey). The word 'monotone' is the root of the word 'monotonous'. And what does a brain do when it is bored? It tunes out, turns off, shuts down and goes to sleep. So 95 per cent of our literate human population is making notes in a manner designed to bore themselves and others to distraction, and to send many of them into a state of unconsciousness. And the method is working. We need only look at libraries in schools, universities, towns and cities around the world. What are half the people doing in those libraries? Sleeping! Our places of learning are becoming giant public bedrooms!

This global 'sleeping sickness' in response to learning is due to the fact that for the last few centuries the vast majority of us have been making notes that use considerably less than half of the capacity of our cerebral cortex. This is because the skills associated with our left and right hemispheres are not able to interact with each other in a way that produces an *upward spiral* of movement and growth. Instead we have saddled our brains with a note-making/taking system that encourages them to reject and forget! The combined disadvantages of these two factors take a heavy toll. Standard note-making/taking systems:

Obscure the key words – Important ideas are conveyed by key words: those words, usually nouns or strong verbs, that bring back sprays of relevant associations whenever they are read or heard. In standard notes these key words often appear on different pages, obscured by the mass of less important words. These factors prevent the brain from making appropriate associations between the key concepts.

Make things difficult to remember – Monotonous (single colour) notes are visually boring. As such, they will be rejected and forgotten. In addition, standard notes often take the form of endless similar-looking lists. The sheer monotony of making such lists puts the brain in a semi-hypnotic trance, making it almost impossible to remember their content.

Waste time – Standard note-making and note-taking systems waste time at all stages by encouraging unnecessary noting and by requiring:

- the reading of unnecessary notes;
- the re-reading of unnecessary notes;
- the searching for key words.

Don't stimulate the brain – By its very nature, the linear presentation of standard notes prevents the brain from making associations, thus counteracting creativity and memory. In addition, especially when faced with list-style notes, the brain constantly has the sense that it has 'come to the end' or 'finished'. This false sense of completion acts almost like a mental narcotic, slowing and stifling our thought processes.

The results of research on note-making/taking

Such findings are supported by many academic studies on note-making/taking, especially those by Dr Howe of Exeter University. Dr Howe's studies aimed to evaluate the effectiveness of different types of noting. Effectiveness was judged by how well students were able to talk from their notes, indicating a full and integrated understanding. They also had to be able to use the notes for review purposes, to provide accurate recall and considered responses in examination conditions where the notes were no longer available. These were the results, from worst to best:

The infinite power and potential of your mind

1 Complete transcript notes given.

2 Complete transcript notes personally made.

3 Sentence summary notes given.

4 Sentence summary notes personally made.

5 Key word notes given. (These sometimes proved to be particularly poor because the person who received them was unable to make appropriate mental associations.)

6 Key word notes personally made.

Howe's studies show that brevity, efficiency and active personal involvement are of crucial importance in successful noting.

The consequences for our brains

Repeated use of inefficient note-making and note-taking systems has a number of consequences for our brains:

- We lose our powers of concentration, as a result of the brain's understandable rebellion against mistreatment.
- We acquire the time-consuming habit of making notes on notes in an attempt to discover the ever more elusive essence of whatever we are studying.
- We experience loss of confidence in our mental abilities and in ourselves.
- We lose the love of learning so evident in young children and those who have been fortunate enough to learn how to learn.
- We suffer from boredom and frustration.
- The harder we work, the less we progress, because we are unwittingly working against ourselves.
- We end up with ever diminishing returns when what we need is a system that produces increasing returns.

A young girl in New York, was at the age of nine, an 'A' student. By the time she was 10 she had become a 'B' student; by the age of 11 a 'C' student; and by the age of 12 a 'D' student, verging on total failure. She, her teachers and her parents were all mystified, as she had been studying as hard, if not harder, every year, and was obviously intelligent.

Her parents arranged for me to meet her. After a long and sad conversation, she suddenly brightened up and said, 'There is one area in which I am doing better and better every year.'

'Which one?' I asked.

'My notes,' she replied.

Her answer hit me like a thunderbolt, for it solved the mystery. In order to do better at school, she had assumed that she must make more and better notes. 'Better', to her, meant 'more sentence-y', as close as possible to verbatim and more traditionally 'neat'. As a result, she was innocently pouring more and more effort into the very activity that was making her misunderstand and forget what she was studying. This method was used deliberately by a Russian called Shereshevsky, who had a perfect memory, to help him to forget! As soon as she realised what she was doing, she was able to use Mind Maps and reverse the trend.

So we see that current systems of note-making and note-taking utilise only a fraction of the brain's enormous learning potential. We also know that the great geniuses used a much greater proportion of the mental capacity that is available to all of us. Armed with this knowledge, we can move forward to the next chapter which outlines in more detail the concept of Radiant Thinking – a clearer, more natural and more efficient way of using our brains.

Radiant Thinking

What happens in your brain when you taste a ripe pear, or smell flowers, listen to music, watch a stream, touch a loved one, or simply reminisce? The answer is both simple and amazingly complex.

Each bit of information entering your brain – every sensation, memory or thought (incorporating every word, number, code, food, fragrance, line, colour, image, beat, note and texture) – can be represented as a central sphere from which radiate tens, hundreds, thousands, *millions* of hooks. Each hook represents an association, and each association has its own infinite array of links and connections. The number of associations you have already 'used' may be thought of as your memory or your brain's personal library. As a result of using this, your brain already contains Mind Maps of information that would have the world's great cartographers gasping in disbelief, could they but see them.

The super bio-computer

Your brain's thinking pattern can be seen as a gigantic 'branching association machine' – a super bio-computer – with lines of thought radiating from a virtually infinite number of data nodes. This structure reflects the neuronal networks that make up the physical architecture of your brain. It also, significantly, mimics what we see in the natural world – in the veins of a leaf, the branches of a tree, or indeed the mighty Amazon river wending its way with its myriad tributaries through the world's largest rainforest. A quick calculation will reveal that your already existing database of items of information, and the associations radiating from them, consists of multiple quadrillions of data associations.

A supernova explosion

Infinite storage

Some people use this vast database as an excuse to stop learning, explaining that their brains are nearly 'full up' and that for this reason they are not going to learn anything new because they need to save the precious, remaining space for the 'really important stuff'. But there is no cause for concern because we now know through neuro-physiological studies that even if your brain were fed ten items of data (each item being a simple word or image) every second for 100 years, it would still have used less than one-tenth of its storage capacity.

This astounding storage capacity is made possible by the almost unbelievable sophistication of the intricate pathways that constitute our metabolic processes. Even a single subsection of one metabolic pathway is amazingly

The infinite power and potential of your mind

complex – however many items of data you have already stored, and however many associations you have already made, your potential to radiate new patterns and combinations of ideas exceeds it by multiple quadrillions. The more you learn and gather new data in an integrated, radiating, organised manner, the easier it is to learn more.

Radiant Thinking (from 'to radiate', meaning 'to spread or move in directions, or from a given centre') refers to associative thought processes that proceed from, or connect to, a central point. The other meanings of 'radiant' are also relevant: 'shining brightly', 'the look of bright eyes beaming with joy and hope' and 'the focal point of a meteoric shower' – similar to the 'burst of thought'.

Mirroring Radiant Thinking

Radiant Thinking reflects the brain's internal structure and processes. The Mind Map is an external mirror of this and allows access to the vast thinking powerhouse of the brain.

A Mind Map always radiates from a central image. Every word and image becomes in itself a subcentre of association, the whole proceeding in a potentially infinite chain of branching patterns linked to the common centre. Although the Mind Map is drawn on a two-dimensional page, it represents a multi-dimensional reality, encompassing space, time and colour.

Sunlight between maple tree branches reflecting through the tree structure, the structure of Mind Maps, and by the sun's radiation, the basic nature of Radiant Thinking.

Before learning how to apply this powerful tool, it is essential to understand the operational principles of the brain that generates it. Radiant Thinking is the natural and virtually automatic way in which all human brains have always functioned. In the evolutionary development of our thinking processes, we have restricted ourselves to single linear beams of the radiation, rather than full, multi-dimensional, Radiant Thinking. A Radiant Thinking brain should express itself in a radiant form which reflects the pattern of its own thought processes. As we shall see in Part 2, the Mind Map is that form.

The infinite power and potential of your mind

Mind mapping is a **creativity and productivity enhancing** technique that can improve the **learning and efficiency of individuals** and organizations. It is a revolutionary system for **capturing ideas and insights** on paper.

Anthony J. Mento and Raymond M. Jones, Loyola College, and Patrick Matinelli, Johns Hopkins University on their executive MBA program

Part 2
Welcome to the Mind Map

The human brain does not think in toolbars and menu lists, it thinks organically like all natural forms – our nervous system or the branches of a tree. To think well, it needs the tools that reflect that natural organic flow. The Mind Map is that tool. It is the next major and inevitable step in the progression from linear ('one-dimensional'), through lateral ('two-dimensional'), to radiant or multi-dimensional thinking.

Armed with the knowledge you have gained about the workings and potential of your brain, Part 2 delves deeper into the twin worlds of words and images to help you unleash extraordinary mental energy through brainstorming and association techniques. This journey lays the foundations for expressing and releasing your mental potential, and leads you on to the core rules and processes of the Mind Map itself.

The Mind Map defined

The Mind Map Is a graphic representation of Radiant Thinking. As we saw in Chapter 3 (and we're about to see in-depth), Radiant Thinking is the process through which the human brain thinks and generates ideas. By capturing and representing Radiant Thinking, the Mind Map creates an external mirror of what is going on inside. Essentially the Mind Map repeats and mimics Radiant Thinking, which, in turn, magnifies the brain's natural function, making it stronger and more powerful.

Characteristics of a Mind Map

A Mind Map is a visual and graphic holistic thinking tool that can be applied to all cognitive functions, especially memory, creativity, learning and all forms of thinking. It has been described as 'the Swiss Army knife for the brain' (see below).

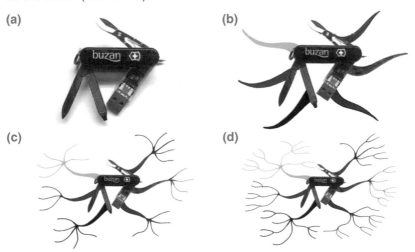

A developing Mind Map from a central image (a) to the Basic Ordering Ideas and first level branches (b), expanding to second level branches (c) and further sub-branches (d)

1 A central image is used to capture the main subject of attention – for example, if you are using a Mind Map to plan a book, you might have a picture of a book in the centre.

2 Branches are created from this image. These are first divided into main themes that flow from the central image, and then subsidiary themes link from the branches.

3 On each branch, a key image or word is used.

Enhance your Mind Map

The more creative you are with a Mind Map the better, so they can (and should) be enriched with colour, more pictures and dimensions (making words and images three-dimensional). You can add special codes to cross-reference branches and add all sorts of features to make it unique to you and your style. By making the Mind Map as visually exciting as possible, you boost its power – our brains respond better to images and colour (more on this later) so the more creative you are with your Mind Map, the better your results will be.

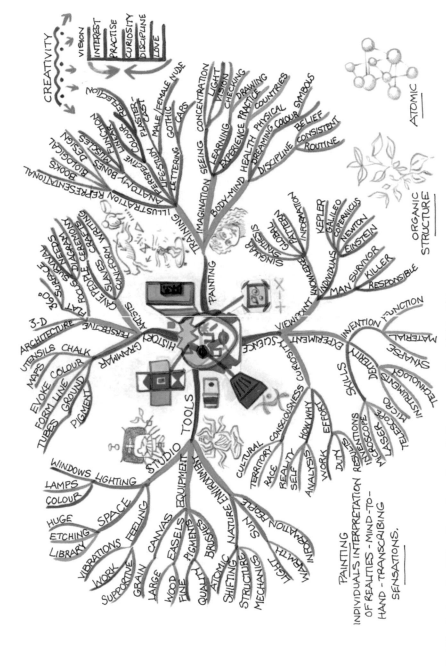

Mind Map by Lorraine Gill on the nature of creativity: a perspective of the artist

Whenever you need to use your brain, you can use a Mind Map to enhance your thinking and memory. Generating ideas, recording and processing information, and running a project are some of the most common uses, and it really can be applied to anything that requires brain power.

Mind Maps are all around us

The clue to the Mind Map's effectiveness lies in its dynamic shape and form. As the Mind Map shoots off from the centre, with its curved lines, symbols, words, colours and images, it reveals itself as a totally natural and organic structure. Every time we look at the veins of a leaf or the branches of a tree, we see nature's 'Mind Maps'. Mind Maps also mimic the myriad synapses and connections of our brain cells and reflect the way we ourselves are created and connected. Like us, the natural world is forever changing and regenerating, and has a communication structure that appears similar to our own. A Mind Map is a natural thinking tool that draws upon the inspiration and effectiveness of these natural structures.

Let's now look at how brainstorming with words and then with images opens up your amazing ability for imagination and association, which itself forms the foundation for creating a true Mind Map.

Dandelion seed head mirrors both the architecture of the Mind Map and the concept of Radiant Thinking

Using words

This chapter explores in depth your brain's Radiant Thinking information-processing system. Through the brainstorming exercises, you will discover the vast potential of your associative machinery as well as gaining an insight into your own uniqueness and that of others.

Mini Mind Map exercise

This quick exercise shows that everyone, whatever their sex, status or nationality, uses Radiant Thinking to link key word associations with key images – instantaneously (see below). This is the basis for all our thinking and this is the basis of Mind Maps.

You are going to complete a mini Mind Map to represent the concept of 'happiness'. You will create ten branches from this word, to carry ten key word associations. This is not a test and should take you no more than one minute. If possible, ask a group of people to do this exercise with you – but do not share your work during the exercise.

Doing the exercise

Write 'happiness' and put a ring around it. From the central image, create ten separate branches. On each branch, write the first words that come into your mind when you think of the concept of happiness. It is important that you put down the first words that come into your head – no matter how ridiculous. If you want to include more words, include these by drawing extra branches.

Analysing the results

Did you find it easy to come up with ten words? Did you go beyond ten? Did you feel a sense of 'flow' as you created more branches?

What most people find is that once you start word associating, one word leads to another and another. A little like following links on the Internet, you read something which leads you on to something else. And so it goes on and on. This is exactly how your brain works, and the Mind Map opens up the channels of association and connection, releasing your potential to think and create freely.

The 'Happiness' exercise

Analysing the results in a group

If you have completed the exercise alone, use my worked example below to compare your words against my words.

In the group, your aim is to find out if you have come up with the same words, associated with happiness, as other people – these words must be exactly the same, so 'sun', for example, is not the same as 'sunshine'.

Before counting up the results, you should each privately predict how many words will be common to all members of the group; how many words common to all but one member; and how many words will have been chosen by only one person.

When you have finished the exercise and made your estimates, compare the words you have noted with everyone else.

Most people predict that there will be many words common to the whole group, with only a few words unique to any individual. Yet, after thousands of trials, we have found that it is rare for there to be even one word common to all members of a group of four.

The more people there are in the group, the less chance there is of any one word being common to all members of the group.

Sample from 'Happiness' exercise

The vast potential of your associative machinery

Consider the fact that every sight, sound, smell, taste or sensation you have ever received – either consciously or paraconsciously – is like a tiny radiant centre with millions of associations emanating from it.

Now think about trying to note down all these associations.

It would be impossible, because every time you noted something you would have a thought about what you had noted. That would be another association, which you would be obliged to note down, and so on, *ad infinitum*. Your human brain can make an infinite number of associations; and your creative thinking potential is similarly infinite. In the average human brain there are multiple quadrillions of 'used' associations. This vast network may be considered not only as your memory or personal reference library, but also as your entire conscious and paraconscious self.

Our extraordinary uniqueness

Every human being is far more unique than we think. The fact that individuals share so few common associations for any given word, image or idea means that we are all magically and eerily different from each other. Your brain contains trillions of associations shared by no one else, past, present or future.

If we find a unique mineral what do we call it? 'a gem', 'priceless', 'a jewel', 'invaluable', 'precious', 'a treasure', 'rare', 'beautiful', 'irreplaceable'. In view of what research has revealed about us, we should start applying these terms to ourselves and our fellow human beings.

Our extraordinary uniqueness has many benefits. For example, in any brainstorming or problem-solving situation, the greater the diversity of ideas the better. Each individual thus becomes an extremely valuable part of the process.

A graphic representation of a single 'unit' of information in the brain

In the wider social context, so-called 'delinquent', 'abnormal' or 'eccentric' behaviour may often now be perceived in a new light as 'appropriate divergence from the norm, leading to increased creativity'. In this way, many apparent social problems may actually turn out to be solutions.

The results of these exercises also highlight the dangers involved in viewing people as groups rather than individuals. Appreciating our uniqueness can help in resolving misunderstandings and conflicts, both personal and social.

Association exercises reveal the unlimited power of every human brain, both those of 'gifted' people and those previously considered to be 'average'. These exercises can liberate billions of people from their self-imposed mental limitations. By simply performing the 'happiness' exercise described in this chapter, anyone can experience an instant explosion in mental power. Understanding that we all associate differently helps us avoid many of the emotional and logical traps that bedevil our attempts to communicate.

An eight-year-old boy in a deprived area of London was considered to be virtually mentally retarded, both by his teacher and by himself. After he had completed the 'happiness' exercise, I asked him whether he could find further associations for any of the ten words he had written down. He paused for a moment, wrote down two, then looked up with the beginnings of a gleam in his eyes and asked, 'Can I keep going?' When I said, 'Yes,' he started tentatively, like someone going into the sea for the first time. Then, with an increasing beat, almost like a drum roll, words and associations started to pour from him. His entire physical posture was transformed into one of eagerness, energy and happiness, as he filled the page, literally shouting, 'I'm smart! I'm smart!' He was right. His education, not he, had been lacking.

If the Radiant Thinking ability of the brain can be applied to the 'left cortical skill' of words, can the same power be applied to the 'right cortical skill' of imagination and images? The next chapter explores this question.

Using images

This chapter, drawing on pioneering brain research, explores why the old adage 'every picture is worth a thousand words' is so important. Together with the practical exercises described here, you'll begin to access the vast store of imaginative skills that lie dormant in 95 per cent of the population.

Word association exercise

To do this and the following exercise, you will need pens and plain, unruled paper. Most people believe that the brain thinks linguistically. We shall see. First, you are going to access a piece of data from that vast database, your brain. You will have no time to think about it in advance. The piece of data you need to locate is a word which will be revealed overleaf, and you need to check the following points:

1 Could you access the word? _____

2 How long did it take to access it? _____

3 What did your brain access? _____

4 Were any colours associated with it? _____

5 Were there any associations radiating
from the piece of data you accessed? _____

6 If so what were they? _____

_____

_____

Now here's the word: A–P–P–L–E

Go through the questions above and write down your answers as quickly as possible *before* reading on.

Analysing the results

1 Undoubtedly you wrote 'yes' – everyone who can read is able to access this data.

2 This should be instantaneous.

3 According to studies, regardless of age, gender, race, primary spoken language and so on, the unanimous response is an image or picture. When you read or 'heard' the word in your head you may have seen the colours red, russet or green – depending on the type of apple. You may have seen its rounded shape. You may have associated the image with a fruit salad, breakfast cereal or a smoothie. The image will have appeared instantaneously, as if from nowhere, and you are unlikely to have spent any time visualising the letters of the word.

4 Yes, for the vast majority of individuals.

5 Again yes. These associations are always individual, linked to the senses.

6 Items can be as varied as a tree to a computer.

What you have discovered through this exercise will affect your own brain-storming, creativity and innovation sessions for the rest of your life.

Thinking and communicating in pictures

For centuries it has been assumed that we think primarily with words. We now realise that we think primarily with images and their associations. The words we use are just the cargo boats that carry our images out from our own brain to other brains.

Whatever the translation – apple, pomme, mela, 苹果, manzana, apfel, μηλo, maçã, Я6пoкo – societies had to work out a way in which they could communicate with each other the idea of that particular fruit. They decided on a 'word' – any sound would have done as long as they agreed that *this* was the sound to convey *this* image. It was always the image that was the centre of the brain's attention.

The incredible power of your brain has been amply demonstrated by this apple imagination game. You have been able to access the word virtually instantaneously – you had to access it and compare it with every other word and all your memories of that word both spoken and written. This is a task that was thrown at you randomly – your brain had to be prepared for any one of an *infinite* number of nouns, and yet it was able to access in nanoseconds the one thrown randomly at it. Impossible! And yet you did it. And every day of your life you do it so brilliantly and continuously that you don't even *notice* it! Again an astonishing and virtually impossible performance.

As we have said, the apple image will have appeared instantaneously, as if from nowhere. So where had that image been before your brain decided to access it? Where were the colours stored? Where were all the associations stored? The image was already stored in your mind; you simply needed to trigger its release. We learn from this that, ultimately, we think in images and not words.

A picture is worth a thousand words

Scientific American magazine published the results of a fascinating experiment carried out by Ralph Haber. The psychologist and expert in visual perception showed a series of 2,560 photographic slides, presenting one image every ten seconds. It took approximately seven hours for all the slides to be reviewed. This viewing time was divided into separate sessions over a period of several days. An hour after the last slide had been shown, the viewers were tested for recognition.

Next, each person was shown 2,560 pairs of slides, in which one slide came from the series they had seen, while the other came from a similar set which they had not seen. On average, the accuracy of their recognition was between 85 and 95 per cent.

Having confirmed the unrivalled accuracy of the brain as a receiving, holding and recalling mechanism, Haber carried out a second experiment to check the brain's ability to recognise at speed. In this experiment one slide was shown every second. The results were identical, indicating that not only does the brain have an extraordinary capacity to imprint and recall, but that it can do so, with no loss of accuracy, at incredibly high speeds.

To test the brain even further, Haber conducted a third experiment in which slides were still presented at the rate of one per second but were all shown as mirror images. Again, the results were identical, indicating that even at high speeds the brain can juggle images in three-dimensional space with no loss of efficiency.

Haber commented: 'These experiments with visual stimuli suggest that recognition of pictures is essentially perfect. The results would probably have been the same if we had used 25,000 pictures instead of 2,500.'

Another researcher, R. S. Nickerson, reported in the *Canadian Journal of Psychology* the results of experiments in which each subject was presented with 600 pictures at the rate of one per second. When tested for recognition immediately after the presentation, average accuracy was a staggering 98 per cent.

Like Haber, Nickerson expanded on his research, increasing the number of pictures from 600 to 10,000. Significantly, Nickerson emphasised that each of his 10,000 pictures were 'vivid' (i.e. striking, memorable images like the ones used in Mind Maps). With the vivid pictures, subjects achieved a recognition accuracy rate of 99.9 per cent. Allowing for some degree of boredom and exhaustion, Nickerson and his colleagues estimated that had their subjects been shown a million pictures, rather than 10,000, they would have recognised 986,300 – an accuracy rate of 98.6 per cent.

The reason why pictures are 'worth a thousand words' is that they make use of a massive range of cortical skills: colour, form, line, dimension, texture, visual rhythm, and especially imagination – a word taken from the Latin *imaginari*, literally meaning 'to picture mentally'. Images trigger a wide range of associations, enhancing creative thinking and memory.

Taking all this into consideration shows how ludicrous it is that over 95 per cent of note-taking/making is done without the benefit of images.

We can *all* draw images

The reason we reject using images is partly our modern overemphasis on the word as the primary vehicle of information, and partly people's (mistaken) belief that they are incapable of creating images. As well as this, it is often said that images are childish and that the power to create images is a talent only a tiny minority of people possess.

We and others, including the artists Dr Betty Edwards and Lorraine Gill, have surveyed opinion in this area. In these surveys, as many as 25 per cent of people said they had no visualisation capability, and more than 90 per cent believed they had a genetic inability to draw or paint in any way. Further research has shown that anyone with a normal brain can learn to draw to good art school level.

The reason why so many people assume that they are incapable of creating images is that, instead of understanding that the brain always succeeds through continued experimentation, they mistake initial failure for fundamental incapacity.

With a more complete understanding of the human brain, we are beginning to realise that a new balance must be established between the skills of the image and those of the word. Computers and PDAs (Personal Digital Assistants, or hand-held computers) today recognise and reflect that link

A Quiver tree reflecting both the organic nature of Mind Maps and Radiant Thinking

and manipulation of words and images together through icons, graphic user interfaces, Facebook, YouTube and virtual worlds such as Second Life. On the personal level, it has given rise to the Mind Map.

Mini Mind Map image exercise

You'll need a large sheet of plain paper and coloured pens for this next exercise.

This image exercise is identical to the 'Happiness' exercise in the last chapter, except that an image is placed in the centre, and on each of the ten branches surrounding the image, 'image associations' are drawn.

In an exercise like this, it is essential for you to overcome any inhibitions you might have about drawing 'bad' images. No matter how 'bad' your images may seem, because of the trial and *success* (not error) nature of the human brain, they will simply form the first experimental stage from which you can only get better and better.

Doing the exercise

A good central image to begin with is 'home', because it provides you with plenty of image association opportunities. Start by drawing an image of what your home looks like to you. This could be anything from a cosy cottage to a desert island – what's important is that this image depicts home to you. From this image draw ten thick branches in different colours and draw one image on each main branch that you associate with home. As you may have done in the word exercise, you may go beyond ten. Include as many as you like, but remember to draw these on new branches, which link to the main branches (see the example on the next page).

Take your time with this exercise and be as colourful as you like – most of all, enjoy it! This is your time to reawaken the artist in you.

Example by Phil Chambers of Mini-Mind Map image exercise using 'home' and the happiness connections that image/idea brings. This is a good example of how to build up your visual 'mental musculature' using a central image with seven key branches. Such visual association exercises will help you unleash the enormous power of your visual cortex, enhance your memory's storing and recalling capabilities through the use of images for emphasis and association, and break down resistance to the use of images in learning. The act of drawing aids mental stimulation and gives aesthetic pleasure through the images themselves

Having explored the importance of images and seen how, through practice, you can build your confidence and skills to draw – remember that *everyone* can draw – it's now time to integrate both words and images and move on to the full Mind Map.

Images and words combined

This chapter introduces you to using both images and words in a Mind Map, as well as to techniques for ordering and structuring your thinking through the Mind Map. To understand truly the process, we'll go inside the mind of a Mind Mapper to see how a Mind Map is put together, 'inside out'.

Harnessing the full range of your cortical skills

The Mind Map harnesses the full range of cortical skills – word, image, number, logic, rhythm, colour and spatial awareness – in a single, uniquely powerful technique. In so doing, it gives you the freedom to roam the infinite expanse of your brain.

In exactly the same way that your ten original words or images radiated from the central concept of 'happiness' each of these ten words or images can also radiate its own associations and can (and should) be a combination of words and images. By 'free-associating' with words and images, you expand and complete your Mind Map.

Infinity exercise

Look at the word-based Mind Map from the 'Happiness' exercise on page 39, and notice that in the extended version on page 52 the original ten words have been written in larger letters, and that the lines on which they rest are thicker than the secondary ones. This serves to emphasise their significance as the ten key concepts which originally sprang to mind. As you make more connections on your Mind Map, you will be increasing the sophistication and power of your memory.

The extended original 'Happiness' exercise, leading to basic verbal mind mapping

By 'free-associating' on each of the ten words or images, connecting the concepts that spring from them with lines and clearly printing single key words on lines which are the same length as the words, you can begin to build a verbal Mind Map 'tree' of associations like the one above. When you look at the illustration you will notice that the original ten words have been written in larger letters, and that the lines on which they rest are bolder.

Hierarchies and categories – your power words

In order to control and apply this vast mental power, you need to structure your thoughts and your Mind Map using hierarchy and categorisation.

The first step is to identify your basic ordering ideas (see also below). Basic ordering ideas are key concepts within which a host of other concepts can be organised. The term 'machines', for example, contains many categories, one of which is 'vehicles'. This generates a further range of lesser categories, one of which is 'cars'. 'Cars' in turn contains a host of types – for example, hatchbacks – which can themselves be subdivided into various models.

'Machines' is a more powerful word than 'vehicle' because it encompasses a larger range of information. 'Machines' both suggests a set of categories and puts them in a hierarchical order lesser to itself.

Likewise this hierarchy can be extended upwards to higher levels. 'Artefacts', for example, could have 'machines' as one of its subjects. These power words or basic ordering ideas are the key to shaping and steering the creative process of association. To put it another way, they are the chapter headings you would use if you were writing a book on the subject.

A classic study carried out by Bower, Clark, Lesgold and Wimzenz in 1969 demonstrated the importance of hierarchies as an aid to memory. In this experiment the subjects were divided into two groups. Each group was shown four cards, with 28 words written on each card.

The people in Group 1 were shown words organised hierarchically. For example, the word 'instrument' was placed at the top, and there were branches down to 'strings' and 'percussion'. On the next level there were branches from the word 'strings' down to 'violin', 'viola' and 'cello', while 'percussion' branched down to 'timpani', 'kettledrum', 'bongo' and so on.

The people in Group 2 were shown exactly the same words but arranged randomly. Both groups were then tested on their ability to recall the words. As you would now expect, those in Group 1, who had been shown words in hierarchies, did far better than those in Group 2, who had been shown random lists of the same words.

Inside the mind of a Mind Mapper

This is your chance to 'get inside' the mind of an experienced Mind Mapper and observe how their ideas take shape through a developing Mind Map. In the process you will have an opportunity to apply all the techniques you have learnt so far, as well as a few new ones.

In the example on page 54 the Mind Mapper starts with a central image that expresses the concept of happiness. They use colour and dimension to enhance the image.

The first basic ordering idea that comes to the mind of our Mind Mapper is 'activities'. This word is printed in large capital letters on a thick, curving line connecting to the centre – the word is the same length as the line.

A quick spray of associations – a sailing boat, a heart, a person running and the word 'sharing' – radiates from the idea of 'activities'.

Our Mind Mapper's brain now flashes to another basic ordering idea – 'people'. This is placed on the left side of the Mind Map, again enlarged and attached to the central image by a thick line. The multiple colours used to write the word reflect the multiple colours of the various races.

Another spray of ideas – 'family', 'friends', 'performers', 'supporters' and 'animals' – radiates from this key word.

Some of these ideas generate more ideas. To 'family' is added 'brother', 'mum', 'dad'. To 'performers' is added 'magicians', 'actors', 'clowns'. And 'supporters' generates 'doctors', 'nurses', 'teachers' and 'coaches'.

The next three thoughts are all basic ordering ideas – 'foods', 'environments' and 'sensations' – and as such are given appropriate status on the

A developing Mind Map exploring one person's notion of happiness

Mind Map. The word 'environments' triggers a picture of mountains and the word 'rural'.

At this point, let's pause to consider the implications of what has been done so far.

Any of the key words or images created so far could be placed at the centre of a new Mind Map, which would again radiate outwards and begin a whole new set of associations.

Bearing this in mind, any Mind Map is potentially infinite. In view of its radiant nature, every key word or image added to a Mind Map itself adds the possibility of a new and greater range of associations, which themselves add the possibilities of new and greater ranges, and so on, *ad infinitum*. This demonstrates yet again the infinite associative and creative nature of every normal human brain.

It also completely contradicts the widely held belief that generating ideas is much more difficult than editing and organising those ideas. If our mind mapping ability is infinite, then the only difficulty is deciding when to stop!

By contrast, linear notes in the form of lists directly oppose the workings of the mind, in that they generate an idea and then deliberately cut it off from the ideas preceding and following it. By continually disassociating each idea from its context, they stunt and cauterise the natural thinking process.

Lists rein in the free-ranging movement of the brain, eventually reducing it to stasis and establishing narrow neural pathways of thought that increasingly reduce the probability of creativity and recall.

The reason why lists do this is that they act in direct opposition to the associative nature of the brain. As an idea is set down it is 'finished with', divorced from the ideas which precede or follow it. This constant guillotining of new thoughts is one of the major factors behind the appalling international statistics on the declining generation of creative ideas.

Returning to our Mind Mapper, we find a momentary mental block has ensued (of course this 'block' is only hypothetical as Mind Maps enable you to overcome such blocks). Mental blocks strike some people dumb for seconds, minutes, hours, years, sometimes even for life. However, once you have understood the infinite associative nature of your brain, you are in a position to help it help itself.

Harnessing the brain's tendency to function in gestalt (or natural tendency for completion), our Mind Mapper simply adds blank lines to the key words on the Mind Map, enticing the brain to 'fill in' the beckoning areas. Once the human brain realises that it can associate anything with anything else, it will almost instantaneously find associations, *especially when given the trigger of an additional stimulus*.

Note here how the Mind Map is based on the true logic of *association*, and not the logic of time. The Mind Map reaches out in any direction and catches any thought from any angle.

From this point on, our Mind Mapper completes the associative network: adding more images; adding second, third and fourth level ideas; linking areas; using appropriate codes; and embracing outlines when a major branch is considered to be complete.

Having generated enough ideas, our Mind Mapper decides to order their ideas further by giving them each a number, thus putting the Mind Map into a chronological sequence should that be necessary.

The full Mind Map

It is the use of hierarchy and categorisation which denotes the full Mind Map – and distinguishes it from the smaller Mind Maps used in exercises earlier. In these, the first ten words or images gained their importance simply by occurring first. In the full Mind Map, they are placed according to their *inherent* importance.

A simple way of identifying the first set of ordering categories off the central idea, the basic ordering ideas, is to ask yourself the following questions:

- What knowledge is required?

- If this were a book, what would its chapter headings be?

- What are my specific objectives?

- What are the most important seven categories in the area under consideration?

- What are my basic questions? 'Why?', 'What?', 'Where?', 'Who?', 'When?', 'How?' often serve remarkably well as major branches in a Mind Map. (They are known as the 'six Ws' or technically as the 'five Ws and one H' and make excellent prompters.)

- What is a larger or more encompassing category into which these fit?

If these questions don't prompt your basic ordering ideas, then try a gestalt approach. Start with the central image or subject and draw between four and seven lines branching out from it. Then ask the above questions again.

Alternatively, you can go back to writing down the first ten words or images that spring to mind, then ask yourself which of them can be combined under more general headings.

The full Mind Map exercise

Skim through this example. Using happiness as your central concept, try to build a complete Mind Map, based on what you have learnt so far. Make sure that your Mind Map uses *both* image and word, basic ordering ideas, hierarchies, categories, sequential numbers, dimensions and codes. Benchmark your Mind Map with the full Mind Map on page 54.

Now you've progressed to the full Mind Map, you're ready to learn more about the fundamental Mind Map guidelines which will help unleash your full thinking and creative potential.

Your Mind Map operations manual

If you buy a new High-Definition TV in a store what do you get with it? An operations manual. If you order a printer online what are you able to download with it? An operations manual. With the human brain what do you get? No operations manual. This chapter gives you the operations manual for mind mapping and your brain. It introduces you to all the techniques and guidelines that will help you create a true, full Mind Map. These guidelines will lead you towards being able to increase massively your mental precision, creativity, power and freedom. Once you have understood and absorbed these Mind Map 'laws', you will be able to develop more rapidly your personal mind mapping style.

The three 'A's of mind mapping

In many ancient Eastern cultures, master teachers traditionally gave new students only three basic instructions: 'obey', 'co-operate' and 'diverge'. Each of these instructions characterised a specific learning stage:

'*Obey*' indicated that the student was to imitate the master, only asking for clarification when necessary. Any other questions were to be noted and raised in the next stage.

'*Co-operate*' referred to the second stage in which the student, having learnt the basic techniques, began to consolidate and integrate the information by asking appropriate questions. At this stage the student would assist the master in analysis and creation.

'Diverge' meant that, having thoroughly learnt all that the master could teach, the student would honour the master by continuing the process of mental evolution. In this way the student could use the master's knowledge as a platform from which to create new insights and paradigms, thus becoming a master of the next generation.

The mind mapping equivalents of these three instructions are the three 'A's:

'Accept' means that, in the first stage, you should set aside any preconceptions you may have about your mental limitations, and follow the mind mapping laws exactly, imitating the models given as precisely as you can.

'Apply' is the second stage, when you have completed the basic training given in this book. At this point, we suggest that you create a minimum of a hundred Mind Maps, applying the laws and recommendations contained in this chapter, developing your personal mind mapping style and experimenting with the different types of Mind Map outlined later in the book. Mind Maps should be used for all aspects of your note-taking and note-making until you feel them to be an entirely natural way of organising your thoughts.

'Adapt' refers to the ongoing development of your own mind mapping skills. Having practised several hundred 'pure' Mind Maps, this is the time to develop the creativity of your own Mind Maps.

Mind Map techniques and guidelines

These are intended to increase, rather than restrict, your mental freedom. In this context, it is important not to confuse order with rigidity, or freedom with chaos. All too often, order is perceived in negative terms as rigid and restrictive. Similarly, freedom is mistaken for chaos and lack of structure. In fact true mental freedom is the ability to create order from chaos.

Emphasis

Emphasis is one of the major factors in improving memory and creativity. All the techniques used for emphasis can also be used for association, and vice versa. The following guidelines enable you to achieve maximum and appropriate emphasis in your Mind Maps.

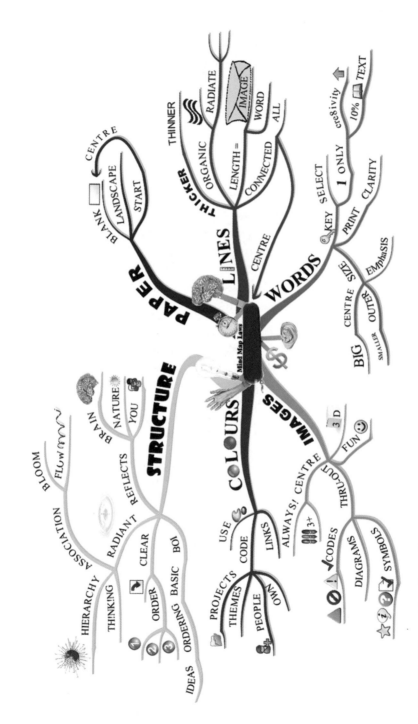

Laws of the Mind Map and how to use them

Always use a central image

An image automatically focuses the eye and the brain. It triggers numerous associations and is astoundingly effective as a memory aid. In addition, an image is attractive – on many levels. It attracts you, it pleases you and it draws your attention to itself. If a particular word (rather than an image) is absolutely central to your Mind Map, the word can be made into an image by using dimension, multiple colours and attractive form.

Use images throughout your Mind Map

Using images wherever possible gives all the benefits described above, as well as creating a stimulating balance between your visual and linguistic cortical skills and improving your visual perception.

If you set aside your fear of being a poor artist, and attempt to draw a butterfly, for example, you may find your first image unsatisfactory. In some instances, you might fail magnificently! The advantage is that you have tried, and the next time you see a butterfly you will want to look at it more closely in order to remember and duplicate it. Thus, by using images in your Mind Maps, you will focus more clearly on real life and will strive to improve your depiction of real objects. This will give you the opportunity to practise Da Vinci's mental mantra of developing your senses by observing, studying and analysing, and finally copying.

Use three or more colours per central image

Colours stimulate memory and creativity, enabling you to escape the danger of monochrome monotony. They add life to your images and make them more attractive.

Use dimension in images and around words

Dimension makes things 'stand out', and whatever stands out is more easily remembered and communicated. Thus the most important elements in your Mind Map can be emphasised by being drawn or written in three dimensions.

Use synaesthesia (the blending of the physical senses)

Wherever possible, you should include in your Mind Maps words or images that refer to the senses of sight, hearing, smell, taste, touch and kinaesthesia (physical sensation). This technique has been used by many of the famous memorisers to remember vast amounts of information, as well as by great writers and poets to make their creative work interesting, entertaining and memorable.

For example, in his epic poem *The Odyssey*, an astounding work of memory, Homer uses the full range of human sensation to convey the excitement and danger of Ulysses' voyage home after the siege of Troy. In the following scene Ulysses has made the mistake of angering Neptune, God of the Sea, who gets his revenge by raising a terrible storm:

As he spoke a sea broke over him with such terrific fury that the raft reeled again, and he was carried overboard a long way off. He let go the helm, and the force of the hurricane was so great that it broke the mast halfway up, and both sail and yard went over into the sea. For a long time Ulysses was under water, and it was all he could do to rise to the surface again, for the clothes Calypso had given him weighed him down; but at last he got his head above water and spat out the bitter brine that was running down his face in streams. In spite of all this, however, he did not lose sight of his raft, but swam as fast as he could towards it, got hold of it and climbed on board again so as to escape drowning. The sea took the raft and tossed it about as Autumn winds whirl thistledown round and round upon a road. It was as though the South, North, East and West winds were all playing battledore and shuttlecock with it at once.

Notice the rhythm, the repetition, the sequencing, the imagery, the appeal to all the senses, the movement, the exaggeration, the colour and feeling, all contained in one masterful and memorable paragraph.

The great memoriser Shereshevsky, known as 'S', used synaesthesia to help him remember virtually every instant of his life. In his book about 'S', *The Mind of a Mnemonist*, the Soviet psychologist Alexander Luria reports:

For 'S', too, it was the meaning of words that was predominantly important. Each word had the effect of summoning up in his mind a graphic image, and what distinguished him from the general run of people was that his images were incomparably more vivid and stable than theirs. Further, his images were invariably linked with synaesthetic components . . .

Use movement

Movement, too, is a major mnemonic technique, and can also be used to advantage in your Mind Maps. Your words, your pictures, your whole Mind Map can move – like the wonderfully memorable Disney and Pixar animations. To make your images move, simply add appropriate visual indicators of movement, using the following techniques.

Use variations of size of printing, line and image

Variation in size is the best way of indicating the relative importance of items in a hierarchy. Expanded size adds emphasis, thereby increasing your probability of recall.

Use organised spacing

Organised spacing increases the clarity of the image, helps in the use of hierarchy and categorisation, leaves the Mind Map 'open' to additions and is aesthetically pleasing.

Use appropriate spacing

Leaving the right amount of space around each item gives your Mind Map order and structure. Taken to its logical conclusion, the space between items can be as important as the items themselves. For example, in Japanese flower arranging, the entire arrangement is based on the space between the flowers.

Association

Association is the other major factor in improving memory and creativity. It is the integrating device our brains use to make sense of our physical experience, the key to human memory and understanding. The power of association will help your brain to explain the depths of any subject.

As already mentioned, any technique used for association can also be used for emphasis, and vice versa.

Use arrows when you want to make connections within and across the branches

Arrows automatically guide your eye to connect one part of a Mind Map with another. They can be uni-directional, multi-headed and varied in size, form and dimension. They give spatial direction to your thoughts.

Use colours

Colour is one of the most powerful tools for enhancing memory and creativity. Choosing specific colours for coding purposes or for specific areas of your Mind Map will give you faster access to the information, improve your memory of the information and increase the number and range of your creative ideas. Such colour codes and symbols can be developed both by individuals and by groups.

Colour is an astonishingly powerful tool for your mind. It allows you to do many things that enhance the power of your thinking: to organise, categorise, highlight, order, code, analyse and learn. In addition, colour stimulates you, engages more of your 'worker' brain cells and, while attracting you, increases your ability to remember. Furthermore, colour boosts your creativity and is fun. If any one of these advantages were the only advantage, colour would still be one of the most powerful thinking tools you have. Use colour in your Mind Maps and your thinking and you and your life will be more colourful!

Use codes

Codes enable you to make instant connections between different parts of your Mind Map, however far apart they may be on the page. These codes can take the form of ticks and crosses, circles, triangles and underlinings, or they can be more elaborate. Codes can also save you a lot of time. For instance, you could use a range of simple codes in all your notes to represent people, projects, elements or processes that frequently recur.

Codes reinforce and enhance categorisation and hierarchy through the simple application of colours, symbols, shapes and images. They can also be used to link source material (such as biographical references) to your Mind Map.

Clarity

Obscurity in thinking veils perception. Aid the flow of your associative thinking and your ability to recall by keeping things clear and easy to understand.

Use only one key word per branch

Each individual word has billions of possible associations. Placing one per line gives you associational freedom, like giving a limb extra joints. Important phrases are not lost and all your options are kept open.

Print your letters

Printed letters have a more defined shape and are therefore easier for your mind to 'photograph'. The extra time spent printing is more than made up for by the advantages of rapid creative association and recall. Printing also encourages brevity, and both upper and lower case letters can be used to show the relative importance of words on your Mind Map.

Make line length equal to word length

This law makes it easier to place words near each other, thus facilitating association. In addition, the space saved enables you to include more information in your Mind Map.

Connect lines

Connecting the lines on your Mind Map enables you to connect the thoughts in your mind. Lines can be transformed into arrows, curves, loops, circles, ovals, triangles, polyhedrons or any of the other shapes from your brain's limitless store.

Make the central lines thicker and organic

Through emphasis, thicker lines immediately signal to your brain the importance of your central ideas. If your Mind Map is at the exploratory stage, you may discover during the mind mapping process that some of the peripheral ideas are actually more important than the central ones. In such cases you can simply thicken the outer lines where appropriate. The organic, curved lines add more visual interest.

Create shapes with the branches in your Mind Map

When a Mind Map branch is completed, it has a unique shape. This unique shape can then trigger the memory of the information contained in that branch. For more advanced mnemonic thinkers, such shapes can become 'living pictures', dramatically enhancing the probability of recall.

Many of us do this naturally as children. For instance, do you ever remember lying outside on a sunny day, looking up at a blue sky dappled with clouds? If you did, the chances are that you looked up at the drifting clouds and thought: 'Oh, there's a sheep!' 'There's a dinosaur!' 'There's a boat!' 'There's a bird' . . . Your brain was creating images from random shapes, thus making the shapes more memorable. In the same way, creating shapes in your Mind Map will enable you to organise many bits of data in a more memorable form. This gathering of data, known as 'chunking', is a well-known mnemonic technique.

Make your images as clear as possible

External clarity encourages internal clarity of thought. A clear Mind Map will also be more elegant, graceful and attractive.

Top ten mind mapping tips

1 Use the right paper and pens

Make sure you use plain paper in landscape format – a landscape page can contain more information than a portrait one and it is more compatible with your wide peripheral vision. Choose an appropriate size of paper for your Mind Map task (better to start big!) and make sure you have lots of colourful pens and highlighters too.

2 Branch off from the centre and follow your brain

The central picture will trigger associated processes in your brain. Follow the hierarchy suggested by your brain. Do not focus too much on having a good structure in the first place. Often, this structure comes naturally by following the free association process. You can freely move from one branch to another. Nothing prevents you from going back to a previous branch to add new ideas to it.

3 Make distinctions

The main branches will contain your basic ordering ideas and therefore need more emphasis. Write them in upper case. Words on secondary branches can be written in upper or lower case.

4 Use key words and pictures

Add on the branch just what you need to retrieve your idea afterwards – one key word or picture is enough. To boost the optimal synergy of both hemispheres, it is important to make sure that all branches, words and pictures form an organic whole. Make your branches just as long as the word on it.

5 Make connections

Take a helicopter view of your Mind Map from time to time. Look for links between different items on your Mind Map. Make these links visible by using connections, images, arrows, codes or colours. Sometimes in your Mind Map the same word or concept will appear on different branches. This is not unnecessary redundancy; it is the Mind Map discovering a new theme that weaves throughout your thinking on the topic. It is useful to highlight such important discoveries. They can lead to paradigm shifts!

6 Have fun

Free your mind (for example, by putting on some music) and don't think 'too hard'. Let your associative mind flow and put your ideas on paper in a very personal and fun way. Fun is a key element of efficient information management. Use everything you can to have fun when making your Mind Map (music, drawings, colours).

▶

7 Copy

Wherever possible, you should copy other good Mind Maps, images and works of art. This is because your brain is designed to learn by copying and then creating new images or concepts from those it has copied. Your reticular activating system (a sophisticated 'sorting station' at the base of your brain) will automatically look out for information that will help you to improve your mind mapping skills.

8 Commit to the absurd

Especially in the initial, creative stages of any Mind Map, all 'absurd' or 'silly' ideas should be recorded, allowing any additional ideas to flow from them. This is because ideas that seem absurd or silly are usually those that are far from the norm. These same ideas often turn out to be the ones that contain the great breakthroughs and new paradigms which are also, by definition, far from the norm.

9 Prepare your workspace/environment

Like your materials, your working environment can evoke in you a negative, neutral or positive response. Your surroundings should be as comfortable as reasonably possible in order to put you in the best frame of mind. Try to use natural light where possible to relax not strain your eyes, and have plenty of fresh air – one of your brain's main foods is oxygen. Ensure that you have a moderate temperature in the room as extremes of temperature will distract you from your work. Furnish the room appropriately by making sure that your chair and desk or table are of the best quality available and that their design allows you to maintain a relaxed, comfortable, upright posture. Good posture increases the supply of blood to your brain, improves perception and enhances mental and physical stamina. In addition, well-designed, attractive furniture will make you want to use your workspace.

Why create pleasing surroundings? Because learning is often associated with punishment, many people paraconsciously make their study or workspace into a prison cell. Make yours a place where you actively want to go, even if you have no particular learning task in mind. A few favourite pictures on the wall, an attractive rug – these little touches can make your workspace a more welcoming, appealing environment.

10 Make it memorable

Your brain is naturally attuned to beauty, so the more beautiful, striking and colourful your Mind Map the more you will remember from it. Therefore, spend time colouring in the branches and images, as well as adding in dimension, flourishes and motifs to the Mind Map overall.

Keep your paper placed horizontally in front of you

The horizontal ('landscape') format gives you more freedom and space to draw your Mind Map than the vertical ('portrait') position. The portrait position has the disadvantage of forcing you to 'bang into' the edges of your note far too soon. A horizontal Mind Map is also easier to read. Inexperienced Mind Mappers often keep the body and pen in the same position while rotating the paper. This may not cause any problems while mind mapping, but re-reading the Mind Map will require physiological contortions that would test the abilities of a yoga master!

Keep your Mind Map as upright as possible

Keeping your Mind Map upright gives your brain easier access to the thoughts expressed. If you keep your lines as close to horizontal as possible, your Mind Map will be much easier to read. Try to keep to a maximum angle of 45°.

Review your Mind Map

If you need an active (as opposed to passive) memory of your Mind Map, perhaps for an exam or a specific project, you should plan to review it at certain times. This will enable you to refine or correct certain areas, fill in any areas which may have been missed and reinforce particularly important associations.

After a one-hour learning period you should ideally review your Mind Map:

- After 10–30 minutes

- After a day

- After a week

- After a month

- After three months

- After six months.

The Mind Map will become part of your ongoing long-term memory.

Speed Mind Maps

Occasionally you should do a speed Mind Map (taking only a few minutes) which summarises all you can recall from your original. When you do one of these fresh Mind Maps you are actually recreating and refreshing your memories, demonstrating yet again that creativity and memory are fundamentally the same mental processes.

If you only check your original Mind Map, your brain remains dependent on the external stimulus of the Mind Map to recognise what it has already done. Producing a fresh Mind Map enables you to check what you can recall without external stimulus. You can then compare the result with your original Mind Map and adjust any errors, inconsistencies or omissions.

In the process of learning and perfecting your Mind Map technique, you will encounter some obstacles along the way, so it's worth looking at these briefly here and considering how you might overcome them.

When you think you no longer have any more spontaneous ideas...

Put your Mind Map down and do something else A new idea often pops up after a break. Add these ideas to your Mind Map and allow them to generate even more new associations.

Start doodling, drawing and colouring Through the process of aesthetically embellishing your Mind Map new ideas will pop up. Recent studies have shown that doodlers are in fact better thinkers! A Mind Map can be seen as a thought-directed 'super-doodle'.

Draw in 'blank' branches Remember our brains are drawn towards completion – by drawing in branches with no words or images, you are enticing your brain into creative action.

The four danger areas

There are four major pitfalls for any Mind Mapper that you need to consider when you're absorbing the guidelines – so you can avoid those pitfalls!

1 Mind Maps that aren't really Mind Maps.

2 The idea that phrases are more meaningful.

3 The idea that a 'messy' Mind Map is no good.

4 A negative emotional reaction to your Mind Map.

All these danger areas can easily be avoided as long as you bear in mind the principles explained below.

1 Mind Maps that aren't really Mind Maps

There are many examples of non Mind Maps purporting to be true Mind Maps, called variously process maps, fishbones, concept maps and flow-charts to name a few. Figures like those below are often created by people at an early stage in mind mapping who have not yet fully absorbed all the Mind Map laws.

At first glance, they look like Mind Maps and seem to obey the fundamental mind mapping principles. There are, however, a number of differences. As both figures develop, their structure becomes increasingly random and monotonous. Furthermore, all the ideas are reduced to the same level and each one becomes disassociated from the others.

Because the laws of clarity, emphasis and association have been neglected, what appeared to be developing into order and structure has in fact resulted in confusion, monotony and chaos.

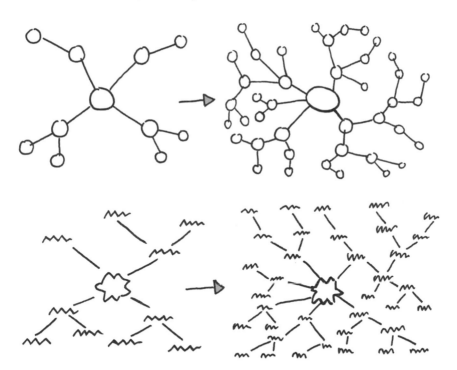

Mind Maps that aren't really Mind Maps. These structures, often named clustering or spider diagrams, lead to confusion, monotony and chaotic thought. Check for yourself just how many cortical skills they include and, more importantly, how many they exclude

2 The idea that phrases are more meaningful

Paradoxically, while appearing to restrict imaginative associations, the one word per branch rule actually gives explosive freedom to the cognitive and other intelligences. How so? Let's say that someone has had a very unhappy afternoon and wishes to make the Mind Map diary entry on this as in the example shown in Figure 8.1.

Initially this may appear to be a perfectly adequate record of an afternoon that was indeed 'very unhappy'. However, on closer examination, a number of disadvantages become clear. First, this note makes it extremely difficult to revise the interpretation of the afternoon. The phrase expresses a fixed concept which is not open to any other possibility.

By contrast, Figure 8.2 breaks the phrase into its individual word meanings, allowing each word the freedom to radiate its own unique associations. The importance of this can be seen even more dramatically in Figure 8.3.

Figure 8.1 Standard phrase noting, which at first glance appears adequate, but which contains dangerous inaccuracies

Figure 8.2 More concise noting, which illustrates the freedom for each word to radiate its own associations

Figure 8.3 Note following the full Mind Map guidelines, which allows the noter to reflect a more comprehensive, true and balanced picture of reality

Taking this a stage further, with the Mind Map on page 74, you can see that the main concept in the afternoon is the concept of happiness, with the major emphasis on the **un** in unhappy. You may have been ill, failed dramatically or received some exceptionally bad news, all of which is true. It is also true that the afternoon contained some positives (the sun may have shone, even if only very briefly!), which the single-word/image rule allows you to record truthfully.

At their worst, negative phrases can wipe out days, years and even decades of people's lives. 'Last year was the worst year of my life', 'My school years were pure hell!', to quote two commonly heard examples.

If such thoughts are constantly repeated they eventually take on the appearance of truth. But they are not true. Certainly, we all experience disappointment and frustration at times. But there are always underlying positive factors – if nothing else, the fact that we are still alive and conscious of being depressed! And of course there is the fact that we still possess the potential for positive change and development.

Using single words in your Mind Maps enables you to see your internal and external environment more clearly and realistically, and therefore to be more 'true' to yourself. It also provides balance, allowing you to see the 'other side' of any issue. It is especially helpful for problem-solving and creative thinking because it opens your mind to all the options. The 'single' rule gives each nexus of your thought the opportunity to explore its own infinite possibilities. It sets you free!

3 The idea that a 'messy' Mind Map is no good

In certain situations, perhaps when you are short of time or you are listening to a rather confusing lecture, you may produce a 'messy'-looking Mind Map. This does not mean it is 'bad'. It is simply a reflection of your state of mind at the time, or of the input your mind was receiving. Your 'messy'-looking Mind Map may lack clarity and beauty but it will still be an accurate record of your mental processes while making it. Consider it simply as a 'first draft' which you can adjust and reorganise into the finished Mind Map. This is especially easy to do with a computer Mind Map.

Realising this can eliminate a lot of guilt and self-denigration. Looking at your Mind Map may help you realise that it was not you but the lecturer you were listening to, or the author of the book you were reading, who was disorganised, messy and confused!

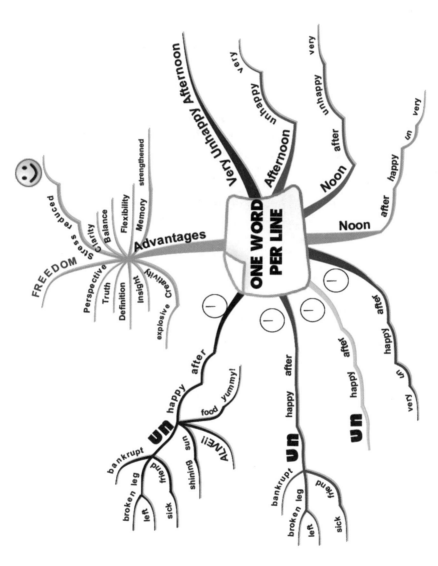

A Mind Map showing the development of a phrase statement step by step to a properly mind-mapped statement (shown on the upper left black branch) with the advantages of applying this process adumbrated on the top green branch

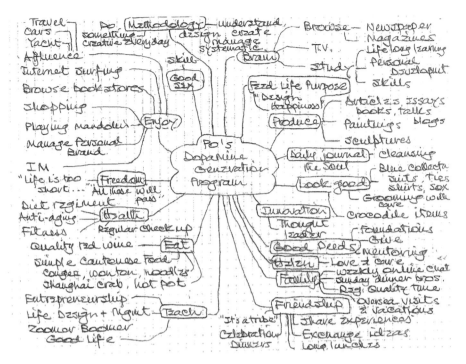

Po Chung's seemingly 'messy' first draft Mind Map

4 A negative emotional reaction to your Mind Map

You may occasionally produce a 'final' Mind Map straight away, but you will more often than not produce a 'first attempt'. If you are disappointed or depressed by the standard of your Mind Map, you should simply remind yourself that it is only a first draft which will require revision before it reaches maturity.

Having read through the techniques, guidelines and tips, and considered all the possible obstacles, it's time to consider how you make your Mind Maps truly your own. The next chapter, 'Mind Maps as art', explains how you can enhance your Mind Maps by using them to express your particular personal combination of skills and characteristics.

Mind Maps as art

Mind Maps provide the ideal opportunity to improve your hand–eye co-ordination and to develop and refine your visual skills. With a little more practice, the image-making skills you have already developed can be used to take your Mind Maps into the realms of art. Such Mind Maps enable your brain to express its own artistic and creative personality.

Why create an art Mind Map?

By spending time creating a more artistic Mind Map, you'll be surprised at how quickly your artistic and visual perception skills improve. This in turn enhances memory and leads to stress reduction, relaxation, self-exploration and ultimately self-confidence. You'll also be developing your creative thinking skills by challenging yourself to come up with creative ideas and images to use in the Mind Map. If you've never spent time on drawing images before, it's an ideal and accessible way for you to get in touch with your inner artist.

How to bring art to your Mind Map

Have a look at the examples of art Mind Maps below and read through the story – it's clear to see just how personal they are to the creator – and you, too, with practice, can develop an individual, personal style.

The essential tools you'll need to create an art Mind Map are colouring pens or pencils, highlighters, large sheets of plain white paper – used in landscape format – and your patient and creative eye. Also, remember from the last chapter that, to really enhance your Mind Map, you should bring different sizes and dimensions to it – release it from the flat page!

Mind Map by Claudius Borer showing how applications of basic principles (the roots) will lead to appropriate fruits!

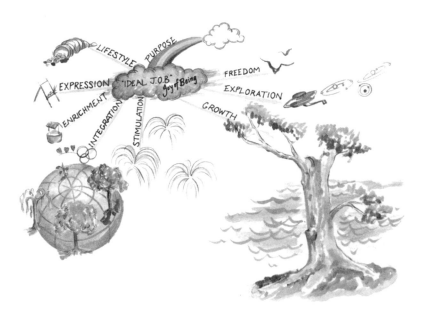

Kathy De Stefano's Mind Map expressing her idea of the ideal job

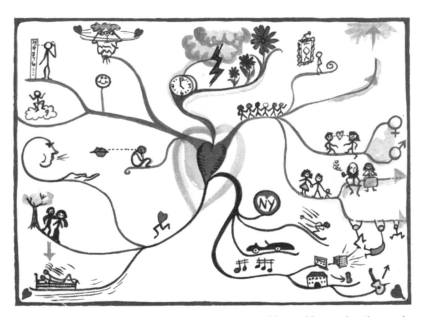

Mind Map by Dr John Geesink, exploring the concept of love without using the word

The artistic Mind Map may take a lot longer than a standard Mind Map, so try to see it as a work in progress – don't rush it – and, most importantly, enjoy it; it's your time to get in touch with your creative self.

It's helpful to create a draft first, with your main branches in place, which you can refer back to as you're developing the images. As we've explored, you'll find that once you draw one image you'll unleash more ideas for images, so don't worry if at first you can't think of what to draw. If you can't 'remember' what something looks like, simply take some time to study it and come back to your Mind Map with this new information – Mind Maps are a great means for you to hone your observation skills.

It's also useful to study other artist's work at this time, to get inspiration. Why not take a trip to an art gallery, look through some art books or simply spend some time to really study shapes and forms. It doesn't matter whether you choose to look at flowers, a building or people; what's important is that you are using the art Mind Map to train your artistic eye.

The extraordinary tree-like Mind Map on page 78 is by Claudius Borer, famous for his Mind Map art. It covers the roots/routes and fruits for growing a business.

The Mind Map at the top of page 79 was drawn by Kathy De Stefano, a marketing consultant, to express her idea of the ideal job. The result is a brilliantly creative work of art as well as a vibrant and creative Mind Map.

The other Mind Map on page 79 was created by Dr John Geesink, an international computer industry consultant. He wanted to express the concept of 'love' artistically, humorously and without using words. People who saw his Mind Map begged him for colour copies!

Like many people worried about the economic environment, C. C. Thum from Singapore realised he needed to expedite an action plan to meet the looming crisis. Creating a Mind Map helped him cope with a big change, the loss of his job. He also produced a Mind Map work of art in the process. See also the world's largest Mind Map on page 200 which was created by a team of mind mappers including C.C. Thum.

C. C. Thum's story

The global financial turmoil has finally impacted me in a direct way. I was not only told I was being retrenched but my last day of service was on the same day in 2008. I couldn't believe that this had happened to me.

I had used Mind Maps before and decided I needed to mind map what was happening to me and how I could cope with the changes. One Mind Map which I had drawn back in 2006 unwittingly came back to guide me. It was a Mind Map of life goals that I had created after attending a Buzan Mind Map seminar. At the time I could visualise my 'retirement' and the action required to achieve the desired outcome. I also realised that I enjoyed mind mapping thoroughly. My job was always given priority and my time spent on mind mapping was rather restricted. Nonetheless, I continued to pursue my dreams and passion.

With the retrenchment and dearth of jobs in the financial industries, my priority has now shifted to mind mapping and actively teaching it to others. The secret to surviving the retrenchment is in the Mind Map. Key ideas are visualised and drawn into the Mind Map. On reflection I realised that Mind Maps actually saved me from constantly worrying about my future and questioning the reasons for retrenching me.

Ulf Ekberg's single-image master Mind Map

The story of a great Mind Map artist

Ulf Ekberg, a Swedish ship's captain who was also an expert on computer systems, took a mind mapping course. Great things were expected of him, for he regularly contributed cartoons to his company's journals, and he had also started studying portrait and landscape painting. At the end of the course, when all the students had to complete their final Mind Maps, Ulf's mind went blank!

Disappointed and frustrated, he went home for the weekend, vowing to devote several hours to completing the course in the grand manner he had dreamed of.

Partly to rid himself of the day's frustrations, he went to work on the large boat he kept in his back garden. It was a freezing winter's day in Stockholm, and as Ulf finished his task he slipped and fell 10 feet on to the ice-hard ground. To his delight, he landed on his feet perfectly. But, as he confidently took a step, he fell to the ground in pain and literally had to crawl back inside. The doctor confirmed that Ulf had two hairline fractures in the heel of each foot, and that he would not be able to walk properly for at least two months.

After his anger at his enforced immobility had subsided, Ulf decided to fulfil one of his lifetime ambitions – to do a painting in the style of Salvador Dali.

He planned to use as his subject a single-image master Mind Map which incorporated everything he had learnt on his course as well as his own interpretations and extrapolations. Among the concepts he wished to include were:

- Introspection – the brain seeing itself seeing itself seeing itself.
- The Roman ideal of *mens sana in corpore sano* ('a healthy mind in a healthy body/a healthy body in a healthy mind').
- Love as an essential element for healthy brain function.
- The brain as synergetic – its parts adding up to more than its whole.
- Time as a variable.
- The mind's ability to create whatever it wishes.
- Juggling as a metaphor for balance and self-control.
- The strong sense of justice found in a highly trained brain.
- The biggest brain on the planet.
- The brain as musical.
- The basic question of existence.
- Einstein's theory of relativity seen in the context of the brain as an infinite association machine.
- Understanding bringing an end to war.
- The brain as magical.
- Mistakes as acceptable and enjoyable parts of the learning process.
- The breaking of all known boundaries.

This first true example of Mind Map art has already been published in limited editions and is rapidly becoming a collectors' item.

Exploring Ekberg's art Mind Map will introduce you to many ideas not yet mentioned in this chapter and will inspire you to develop your personal mind mapping style even further.

Now you are ready to combine your personal style with the guiding principles you have learnt for mind mapping. In the next part you can begin to explore the many thought-processing tasks which can be successfully accomplished using Mind Maps.

Like any muscle, to be powerful, **the human brain** needs training. The **Mind Map** provides your brain with the perfect 'work out', boosting your **thinking, creativity and memory skills**. As with all training, the more you do it, the **better you become**.

Tony Buzan

Part 3
Fundamental applications

This third part is your first step into the application of the Mind Map. Here we focus on the fundamental applications – memory, creativity, decision-making and organising other people's ideas.

As the Mind Map started primarily as a memory tool, we start here, exploring why the Mind Map is such a powerful memory aid and how it links back to an ancient memory technique called 'loci'. We move on to look at how Mind Maps can produce easily twice as many ideas as traditional brainstorming methods and how you can supercharge your creative thinking. The last two chapters of Part 3 take Mind Maps into the realms of decision-making and organising information, preparing you for Part 4 of the book, in which we will see how Mind Maps can be applied to all aspects of your life.

Mind Maps for memory

If you type the word 'memory' into a search engine, you get hundreds of millions of hits, referring you to pages where you can either read about or even train your memory. These pages are all linked by the fact that memory needs to be worked on and trained to perform well. If you don't work on your memory, as with your body, it becomes weak. This chapter introduces you to how Mind Maps are the perfect training tool to flex and build the muscles of your memory.

Mind Maps in history

The Mind Map has a special relationship to memory. It was during research into recall that the Mind Map was first conceived. The Mind Map also links back to a powerful and ancient memory technique. Back in 477 BC a Greek poet named Simonides of Ceos devised a memory technique called the 'method of "loci"', 'loci' meaning 'place'. With little writing material available, it was common for orators and others to memorise their speeches or other items by imagining a journey, placing the items to be remembered along the route and then mentally tracing their steps to recall each item. Imagination and association were the memory triggers. The Romans took the method up, and the oral tradition survived into the Renaissance, but was sadly neglected with the arrival of the printing press. Now, many years on, the Mind Map draws on similar principles. Each branch on the Mind Map is essentially a 'room' in which many things are stored, and our imagination and association are used to trigger memory.

Mind Maps utilise all our cortical skills and activate the brain on all levels, making it more alert and skilful at remembering. The attractiveness of Mind Maps makes the brain want to return to them, and again encourages the probability of spontaneous recall.

How Mind Maps improve your memory

Store information in 'relaxed concentration'

Do you remember a time when you were sitting an exam and there was this one question to which you could not recall the answer? And yet you knew that you knew it? The harder you concentrated on finding the answer, the more it went into 'hiding' in your brain. That is until you 'relaxed' your brain and then – without effort – it popped up, unfortunately, often too late. Scientists now know that a brain under constant stress produces the wrong chemicals for effective recall. Relaxation is a key to retrieval and also creation of data. Mind Maps, because of how we build and engage with them, are the ideal means to relax your brain, empowering you to think and remember.

Cluster data

Most people who use linear note-taking during a meeting, a course or a presentation (if the speed at which information comes is not too fast) tend to insert some structure into their notes. That is definitely necessary for the brain. On average, it can take in five to seven non-linked elements before becoming stressed. Anything more than that needs to be clustered in order to be assimilated. However, the main limitation of the linear note-taking model is that the clustering is only reflected through a numbering system and sometimes indentation. Mind Maps offer far more elements to visualise clustering: colour; shape; connections; structure; different fonts, etc. In addition to these elements, you can cluster and still stick to one page (which provides an overview) far more easily with a Mind Map.

Repeat data

Needless to say, repetition assists in recalling information. By 'reviewing' information, the synaptic connections in your brain involved in a particular storage process are being reactivated. This makes these connections stronger and easier to access. This need for repetition is met by Mind Maps in two ways:

1 When you create a Mind Map, the data already processed remains in eye-sight all the time, since Mind Maps consist of only one page. This means that your brain is constantly repeating these data.

2 Mind Maps are condensed and inviting to look at. The main elements of memory include imagination, colour, shape, association, structure and loci (specific locations). All of these memory enhancers are the essential components of a Mind Map. Linear notes, by contrast, are monochromatic and anti-mnemonic.

Memorising with Mind Maps

There are many general memorising applications for Mind Maps, such as recalling pieces of information, dreams, historical events and general lists of 'things to do' (see examples overleaf).

One particularly useful application is searching for a 'lost' memory – perhaps a person's name or the whereabouts of an object. In such cases, focusing on the missing item is usually counter-productive because 'it' has gone, and in focusing on 'it' you are focusing on an absence or nothingness. Bearing in mind the associative power of your mind, leave the centre of your Mind Map blank, and surround it with words and images associated with the absent centre. For example, if the 'missing' centre is the name of a person, the major surrounding branches would include sex, age, appearance, family, voice, hobbies, profession, and where you first and last met. In this way you dramatically increase the probability of your brain re-accessing the centre from its memory banks.

If you find it inconvenient to create a physical Mind Map to retrieve a 'missing' memory, you can simply visualise an internal screen on which you create the same sort of Mind Map.

Mind Maps are essentially mega mnemonic devices for storing and retrieving information. But they go beyond that by sparking ideas and association to create new knowledge patterns. They become, as we shall see in the next chapter, creative thinking devices.

Mind Maps are very useful for recalling 'things to do'

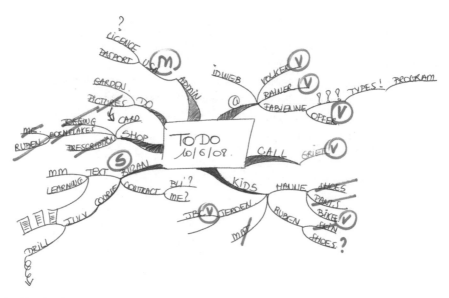

Another 'to do' Mind Map created by Buzan Master Trainer Hilde Jaspaert: the cross-hatched 'T' symbolises a calendar, the heart shape and smileys represent things to do for those Hilde loves, the 'tick off' sign reminds her that the purpose of the Mind Map is to 'get things done', the non-smiley reminds her to include things she doesn't like, the phones are calls to make and the '@' is for emails

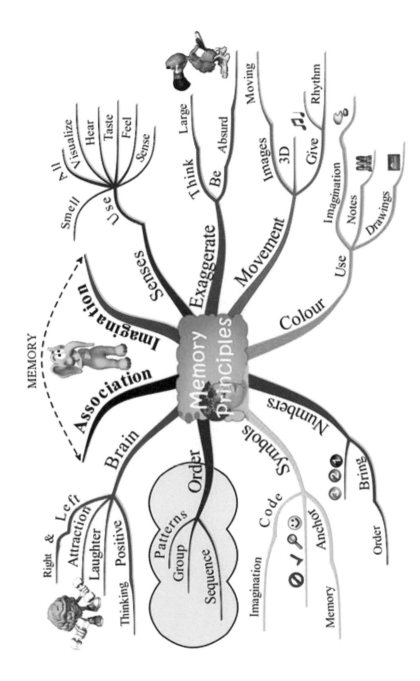

Memory principles Mind Map

Mind Maps for creative thinking

In this chapter our focus is on using Mind Maps for creative thinking. You will discover why Mind Maps are so startlingly effective in this area, and how you can use them to stretch and expand your own creative thinking.

What is creative thinking?

In psychological literature, especially in the testing manuals on creative thinking by E. Paul Torrance (known as the 'father of creativity', with nearly 60 years of research, his findings set the benchmark method for quantifying creativity), flexibility has been identified as a vital element in creative thinking. Other important factors include:

- Being able to create new associations from existing ideas.
- Combining unusual elements together.
- Rearranging and linking pre-existing ideas.
- Reversing and turning existing ideas on their head.

Different colours, shapes and dimensions help us think creatively as they engage our emotions and aesthetic eye – vital to the creative process.

Why use Mind Maps for creative thinking?

Mind Maps utilise *all* these defined creative thinking skills. When we create a Mind Map, we generate mental energy that fuels us to hunt for ideas that normally lie on the periphery of our thinking. Because they are a pleasure to create, Mind Maps encourage a playful side of us, which frees our thinking and opens up the possibility of creating endless ideas. Once we've created a Mind Map, we can view many elements all at once, increasing the probability of creative association and seeing new connections.

Mind Maps boost creative thinking by helping us to:

- Explore *all* the creative possibilities of a given subject.

- Clear the mind of previous assumptions about the subject.

- Generate ideas that result in specific action being taken.

- Create new conceptual frameworks.

- Capture and develop 'flashes' of insight.

- Plan creatively.

Creative thinking may mean simply the realisation that there is no particular virtue in doing things the way they have always been done.

RUDOLF FLESCH

Supercharge your creative thinking

Whilst Mind Maps, in general, are a creative thinking tool, there is a specific creative thinking process you can apply, using Mind Maps, that can produce at least twice as many creative ideas as traditional brainstorming. There are five stages to this.

1 The quick-fire Mind Map burst

Begin by drawing a stimulating central image. Your image should be placed in the centre of a large blank page, and from it should radiate every idea that comes into your mind when you think of that subject. For no more than 20 minutes you should let the ideas flow as fast as possible.

Having to work at speed unchains your brain from its habitual thinking patterns, and encourages new and often apparently absurd ideas. These apparently absurd ideas should always be left in, because they contain the keys to new perspectives and the breaking of old and restrictive habits.

The reason for the page being as large as possible is to be found in the maxim: 'a Mind Map will expand to fill the space available'. In creative thinking, you need as much space as possible in order to entice your brain to pour out more and more ideas. Your brain will leap at the opportunity to fill whatever space is provided. In all creativity, provide it with as large a sheet as possible.

2 Reconstruction and revision

Have a short break, allowing your brain to rest and begin to integrate the ideas generated so far. Now make a new Mind Map, in which you identify the major branches (basic ordering ideas) and build hierarchies within these branches, combining and categorising ideas as you go along, finding new associations. Consider any ideas that you initially thought were 'stupid' or 'absurd' and see if they fit in the context of the Mind Map – the less conventional an idea, the better it often turns out to be!

You may notice similar or even identical concepts appearing on different branches at the outer boundaries of your Mind Map. These should not be dismissed as unnecessary repetitions. They are fundamentally 'different' in that they are attaching themselves to different branches radiating from the central image. These repetitions reflect the importance of ideas which are buried deep within your store of knowledge, but which actually influence every aspect of your thinking. To give such concepts their appropriate mental and visual weight, you should underline them on their second appearance; outline them with a geometric shape on their third appearance; and, if they recur a fourth time, box them in three-dimensional shapes.

Linking these related three-dimensional areas on your Mind Map can create a new mental framework, leading to the flash of insight that occurs when old facts are seen from a new perspective. Such a shift represents a massive and instantaneous reorganisation of entire structures of thought. You will have begun your journey, with the help of your companion Mind Map, to the discovery of new paradigms of thought.

In a sense, this type of Mind Map may appear to be 'breaking the rules', in that the central image and major branches no longer have central importance. However, far from breaking the rules, such a Mind Map is using them to the full, particularly those of emphasis and imagery. A new idea discovered and repeated on the boundaries of thought may become the new centre. Following your brain's search-and-find workings, the Mind Map explores the furthest reaches of your current thought in search of a new centre to replace the old. And in due course this new centre will itself be replaced by a new and even more advanced concept. This is the new paradigm for which you've been searching.

3 Incubation

After completing your second Mind Map, take a longer break – really let your mind settle. Do something different – try going for a walk, listening to music, having a bath. Creative insights often come when your brain is relaxed and peaceful. This is because such states of mind allow the Radiant Thinking process to spread to the farthest reaches of the parabrain, increasing the probability of mental breakthroughs.

The great creative thinkers have used this method throughout history. Einstein instructed his students to include incubation as a necessary part of all their cogitations, and Kekule, who discovered the benzene ring, scheduled incubation/focused daydreaming periods into his daily work programme.

4 Second reconstruction and revision

After incubation, your brain will have a fresh perspective on your first and second Mind Map. It is helpful at this point to do another quick-fire Mind Map burst to consolidate the results of this integration.

Now you need to consider all the information gathered and integrated in stages 1, 2 and 3, along with your second quick-fire Mind Map, in order to make a final, comprehensive Mind Map.

5 The solution

At this stage you need to search for the solution, decision or realisation which was your original creative thinking goal. This often involves linking disparate elements in your final Mind Map, leading to major new insights and breakthroughs.

> *Genius . . . is the capacity to see ten things where the ordinary man sees one, and where the man of talent sees two or three, plus the ability to register that multiple perception in the material of his art.*
>
> EZRA POUND

Mind mapping to gain new perspectives

During deep and prolonged creative thinking, if new insights have been gained at the first reconstruction and revision stage, incubation may produce a new perspective on the collective insights, known as a paradigm shift. The Mind Map on page 98 by Benjamin Zander, Conductor of the Boston Philharmonic Orchestra, is the result of such a process. The Mind

Map reflects Zander's startlingly new approach to Beethoven's Symphony No. 9, an approach that was the result of years of study, internal mind mapping and intense incubation.

In Chapters 10 and 11 you have been introduced to the two most important ways the Mind Map can be applied, quite literally, to 'feed' your brain. Now let's look at how you can use Mind Maps to organise ideas and help you make better decisions.

Ultimately creative Mind Map on the creation theme with Beethoven's ninth symphony, by Benjamin Zander, Conductor of the Boston Philharmonic Orchestra

Mind Maps for making decisions

The Mind Map is a particularly useful tool to review your options before taking decisions. This chapter will show you how to use Mind Maps to set out your needs, desires, priorities and constraints, helping you make decisions based on a clearer view of the issues involved.

Why use Mind Maps for decisions?

Mind Maps allow your brain to assimilate immediately a whole range of complex and interrelated items of information, bringing all the issues into clear focus. They give your brain a pre-structured framework for association, ensuring that all the relevant elements are taken into consideration. The colours and images in Mind Maps bring, additionally, vital emotional responses into the decision and help to highlight the major points of comparison.

You'll find that you generate a greater number of specific items than any list method and that the mind mapping process itself often results in or triggers a decision. By clearly reflecting the internal decision-making process, Mind Maps help you remain focused on all the key elements relevant to any decision.

In making decisions, the Mind Map helps you to balance competing factors. For example, if you're deciding whether to buy a second-hand car or a new car, you can use a Mind Map to help you highlight key trade-offs, such as financial saving versus reliability and durability.

Making simple decisions

A simple decision is known as a dyadic decision (derived from the Latin *dyas*, meaning 'two'). Dyadic decisions are the first stage in creating order.

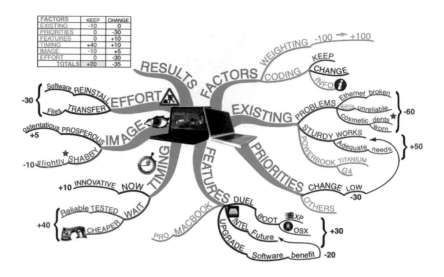

FACTORS	KEEP	CHANGE
EXISTING	-10	0
PRIORITIES	0	-30
FEATURES	0	+10
TIMING	+40	+10
IMAGE	-10	+5
EFFORT	0	-30
TOTALS	+20	-35

Mind Map for a dyadic decision for choosing a new laptop computer

They can be broadly categorised as evaluation decisions, and they involve simple choices such as: yes/no, better/worse, stronger/weaker, more effective/less effective, more efficient/less efficient, more expensive/less expensive.

To create a Mind Map to help you make a dyadic decision, do the following:

1 Draw an image in the centre that represents what the decision is about. This Mind Map example highlights the decision-making process for choosing a new computer.

2 Draw the main branches out of this, the basic ordering ideas, that reflect the key decision-making processes.

3 From these main branches, allow your mind to flow freely, creating lesser branches, with words and images to capture whatever thoughts and emotions spring to mind related to the decision. Remember to use colour and dimension to help capture your emotions – contrary to widespread opinion, emotions are a key component in decision-making. By representing them clearly in a Mind Map, they will help you access your intuitive skills.

Once all the relevant information, thoughts and emotions have been collated on to the Mind Map, there are five major methods for making a dyadic choice.

1 Process-generated

In many cases the process of mind mapping itself generates the solution. As the brain gets an overview of all the data it has gathered there is a sudden 'aha!' realisation which effectively concludes the decision-making process.

2 Number-weighting

If, after completion of the Mind Map, the decision is still not clear, the number-weighting method can be used. In this method, each specific key word on either side of the Mind Map is given a number from 1 to 100 according to its importance. When each item has been given a number, the 'scores' are added up, first for the 'yes' side and then for the 'no' side. The highest total 'wins'.

3 Intuition/superlogic

If neither the first nor the second method has generated a decision, a choice can be made on the basis of intuition or 'gut feel'. Intuition is a much-maligned mental skill which I prefer to define as a 'superlogic'. Your brain uses superlogic in order to consider its vast data bank (consisting of many billions of items gained from previous experience) in relation to any decision you have to make.

'Superlogic', in relation to decision-making, can be seen as a flash your brain completes, considering trillions of possibilities and permutations, in order to arrive at a mathematically precise estimate of probable success, which might be subconsciously expressed as follows:

Having considered the virtually infinite database of your previous life, and integrated that with the trillion items of data you have presented me with in the current decision-making situation, my current estimate of your probability of success is 83.7862 per cent.

The result of this massive calculation registers in the brain, is translated into a biological reaction and is interpreted by the individual as a simple 'gut feel'. Studies at Harvard Business School have found that managers and CEOs of national and multinational organisations attributed 80 per cent of their success to acting on intuition or 'gut feel'. The Mind Map is especially useful for this form of super-thinking, in that it gives your brain a wider range of information on which to base its calculations.

4 Incubation

A fourth method is simply to allow your brain to incubate an idea. In other words, having completed your decision-making Mind Map, you allow your brain to relax. It is at times of rest and solitude that our brains harmonise and integrate all the data they have received and when we often make our most important and accurate decisions. This is because relaxation releases the gigantic powers of the 'parabrain' – the 99 per cent of our unused mental ability, including that which is often called 'the paraconscious'. For example, many people report suddenly remembering where something is, suddenly having creative ideas or suddenly realising that they need to make a particular choice while lying in the bath. This technique is how your brain harmonises and integrates, and through this process tends to make its most meaningful and accurate decisions.

5 If the weightings are equal

If you have completed your Mind Map and none of the previous methods has generated a decision, there must be an equal weighting between 'yes' and 'no'. In a case like this, either choice will be satisfactory, and you may find it useful simply to toss a coin (the ultimate dyadic device) – heads for one option, tails for the other. During the coin-tossing you should monitor your emotions very carefully, in case you find that you really *do* have a preference. You may think you have decided that the choice is equal but your 'parabrain' may already have made its decision.

If the coin shows heads, and your first reaction is one of disappointment or relief then your true feelings will finally be revealed and you will be able to make the appropriate choice.

Indecision

If all of the above decision-making methods fail, your brain will undergo a subtle shift from the dyadic (two-option) choice to a triadic (three-option) choice. The decision is no longer simply 'yes' or 'no'. It is now:

1 Yes.

2 No.

3 Continue thinking about the choice.

The third option is not only counter-productive, it becomes more so the longer it is maintained, as it takes up mental energy. The simplest solution to this problem is to decide not to make the third decision. The basic principle here is that it is more fruitful to have made some decision and to be implementing it than to be in a state of vacillating paralysis.

Critical thinking exercise

Like all forms of thinking, dyadic decision-making requires training. Practise your decision-making skills by asking yourself the following questions:

Should I buy item X? Should I learn subject X? Should I change personal characteristic X? Should I join organisation X? Should I go to country/city X?

In the following 'object X' exercise, the basic idea is to find basic ordering ideas without having any data – in other words, to construct a set of questions that you can address to any object and which, as a set of enquiries, can serve as the basis for a full Mind Map once the object is identified. This exercise can also be done to help you analyse a question before you attempt to answer it. In the 'object X' exercise Mind Map, the main branches are explained as follows:

- **History**: What are its origins? How did it develop?

- **Structure**: What form does it take? How is it constructed? These enquiries can range from the molecular to the architectural.

- **Function**: How does it work? What are its dynamics?

- **Role**: What does it do (a) in the natural world and (b) in the human world?

- **Classification**: How does it relate to other things? This can range from very general animal, vegetable, mineral type questions to specific classifications such as species or the table of elements.

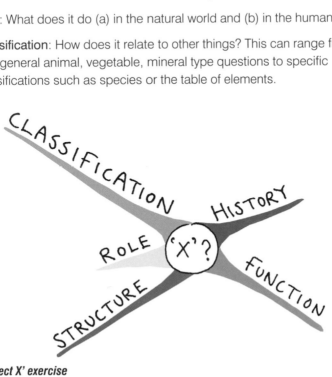

The 'object X' exercise

You might like to try this exercise with one of the following 'object X' suggestions: horse, car, carbon, Spain, sun, God, stone, book, TV. Of course you can use anything else of your choosing. When you have finished this exercise, see if you can improve upon the basic set of Mind Map ideas.

You can also create dyadic Mind Maps on areas of public debate, such as religion, politics, morality, the professions or the educational system.

The point of the exercise is that you are developing your thinking skills by evaluating something without being given any information, and then organising it into areas of importance. If you keep stretching your critical thinking skills and using Mind Maps to capture your thoughts, making clear, well-considered decisions will become as automatic and natural as breathing.

Making complicated decisions

Having familiarised yourself with basic decision-making Mind Maps, you are now ready to make the transition to mind mapping more complex decisions and organising your own ideas. Before you do this, try the following imagination exercise to get your brain to help you come up with more complicated ideas and associations for your Mind Maps.

Exercise

Specify an object for each item on the list, and try choosing some 'absurd' objects in order to boost your imagination, memory and creative thinking abilities all at the same time. The next step is to do a very quick, speed Mind Map for each one, choosing no more than seven major reasons why each item would be fun. This is an excellent way of improving your ability to select relevant basic ordering ideas quickly.

Imagine, and then Mind Map, why it would be fun to:

- Go out with a . . .

- Buy a . . .

- Learn a . . .

- Change a . . .

- Believe a . . .

- Withdraw from a . . .

- Begin a . . .

- Create a . . .

- Finish a . . .

Now you can progress to more complex hierarchies and a greater number of basic ordering ideas than in the simple decision-making models you have worked through. Multi-branched Mind Maps can be used for most descriptive, analytic and evaluative tasks as we progress from basic decision-making examples.

Mind Maps, as we've explored in earlier chapters, can have any number of major branches, even when dealing with dyadic decisions of yes/no and one of two (or three) possible outcomes. The average number of branches or basic ordering ideas is between three and seven. This is because, as we saw in Chapter 10 (page 88), the average brain cannot hold more than seven major items of information in its short-term memory.

Coming up with your basic ordering ideas

You should therefore aim to select the minimum number of basic ordering ideas that will truly embrace your subject, using them as a way of breaking the information up into manageable chunks, like those chapter titles in a book. The following groups of basic ordering ideas have been found to be particularly useful in developing true Mind Maps:

- Basic questions – how/when/where/why/what/who/which?
- Divisions – chapters/lessons/themes
- Properties – characteristics of things
- History – chronological sequence of events
- Structure – forms of things
- Function – what things do
- Process – how things work
- Evaluation – how good/worthwhile/beneficial things are
- Classification – how things are related to each other
- Definitions – what things mean
- Personalities – what roles/characters people have.

To create a Mind Map to help you make a more complicated decision, do the following:

1 Draw an image in the centre that represents what the decision is about. For example, whether to go to university or not (see Mind Map on page 107).

2 Draw the main branches out of this (the basic ordering ideas) that reflect the full range of choices available – for example, university, gap year, employment, live, transport. This process immediately clarifies the range of choices to be made, highlighting the key trade-offs which will govern the decision.

3 From each basic ordering idea, allow your mind to freely associate more ideas, creating lesser branches from the basic ordering ideas.

The Mind Map does not make the decision itself, it presents a 'smorgasbord' of choices from which the most appropriate decision can be taken.

Now that you have learnt how Mind Maps can help you clarify your own thoughts when confronting decisions, the next and final step in this part is to look at how you can apply Mind Maps to ordering other people's thoughts and ideas. The vital and enjoyable art of note-taking, traditionally the bane of many people's lives, is the subject of the next chapter.

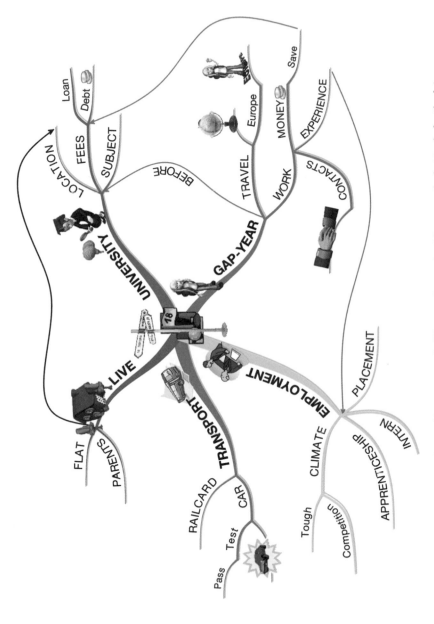

Mind Map to help work through complex decision-making process, in this case for a school leaver and what to do for the future

Mind Maps for organising other people's ideas (note taking)

This chapter looks at how you can use Mind Maps to organise other people's ideas. Linear note-taking is the traditional way to capture other people's ideas from presentations, lectures, courses, books, the Internet and other media, for example, here you'll find out how to replace linear note-taking with Mind Map 'notes' – and you'll be amazed at how much more effective Mind Maps are for note-taking.

Why use Mind Maps for taking notes?

At a glance, you can see what's important and what's not, and the links between key concepts are immediately identifiable. Because the Mind Map is on one page and so clearly structured, you can review information much more quickly and remember it much better too, as each Mind Map is unique and will therefore stand out in your memory. The Mind Map is a permanent and evolving record of your learning that you can add to and embellish whenever you like.

The four main functions of notes

Mnemonic – Analytic – Creative – Conversational

Mnemonic

Sadly, most students in school and universities around the world seem to think that notes are nothing more than a memory aid. Their only concern is that their notes should enable them to remember what they have heard and read, just long enough to pass their exams, after which the information can be happily forgotten. As we have seen, memory is indeed a major factor, but by no means the only one. Other functions, such as analysis and creativity, are equally important.

The Mind Map is a particularly effective mnemonic device for all the reasons outlined earlier. As a note-taking technique, it has none of the disadvantages of standard linear note-taking, as described in Chapter 2. Instead, it offers all the advantages of a method that works in harmony with your brain, utilising and releasing the full range of your capabilities.

Analytic

When taking notes from lectures or from written material, it is essential first of all to identify the underlying structure of the information being presented. Mind Maps can help you extract the basic ordering ideas and hierarchies from linear information.

Creative

Mind Maps combine notes taken from the external environment (lectures, books, journals and the media) with notes made from the internal environment – your own thoughts (decision-making, analysis and creative thought). The best notes will not only help you remember and analyse information, they will also act as a springboard for creative thought.

Conversational

When you take Mind Map notes from a lecture or book, your notes should record all the relevant information from that source. Ideally, they should also include the spontaneous thoughts that arise in your mind while listening to the lecture or reading the book. In other words, your Mind Map should reflect the conversation between your intellect and that of the speaker or author. Special colour or symbol codes can be used to distinguish your own contribution to the exchange of ideas.

If the lecture or book happens to be badly organised or badly expressed, your Mind Map will reflect that lack of clarity. This may result in a messy-looking Mind Map, it will also reveal the source of the confusion. This gives you a better grip on the situation than linear note-takers, who disguise their confusion in pages of neatly written but functionally useless lines and lists. The Mind Map thus becomes a powerful tool for gathering information from others *and* for assessing the quality of their thinking and ability to relate it to your personal needs and goals.

Mind mapping notes from a book

It is important for you to organise your approach so that you can build up a clearly structured Mind Map as your note-taking progresses. Follow the process below to learn how to use Mind Maps to take notes from a book or other text-based source:

1 Quickly *browse* or look through the entire book, web entry or article, getting a general feel for the way it is organised.

2 Work out the length of *time* to be spent studying, and determine the amount of material to be covered in that time.

3 Mind map what you already *know* in that subject area in order to establish associative mental 'grappling hooks'.

4 Define, with a mini Mind Map, your *aims* and *objectives* for this study session, and complete a different Mind Map of all the questions that need to be answered.

5 Take an *overview* of the text, looking at the table of contents, major headings, results, conclusions, summaries, major illustrations or graphs, and any other important elements which catch your eye. This process will give you the central image and main branches (or basic ordering ideas) of your new Mind Map of the text.

6 Now move on to the *preview*, looking at all the material not covered in the overview, particularly the beginnings and ends of paragraphs, sections and chapters, where the essential information tends to be concentrated. Add to your Mind Map.

7 The next stage is the *inview*, in which you fill in the bulk of the learning puzzle, still skipping over any major problem areas. Having familiarised yourself with the rest of the text, you should now find it much easier to understand these passages and bulk out your Mind Map.

8 Finally, there is the review stage, in which you go back over the difficult areas you skipped in the earlier stages and look back over the text to answer any remaining questions or fulfil any remaining objectives. At this point you should complete your Mind Map notes.

The process can be likened to building up a jigsaw puzzle, beginning by look-ing at the complete picture on the box, then putting in the corners and outside edges, and gradually filling in the middle until you have a complete replica.

Revising a novel

The Mind Map below was produced by a father to help his daughter revise a novel for her university entrance examinations in English literature. When confronted with a structure as complex as the novel, it is an enormous advantage for the brain to be able to refer to this type of mental 'grid', which sets out the major literary elements in the novel. This type of Mind Map enables the reader to extract the essence of any text more accurately and comprehensively.

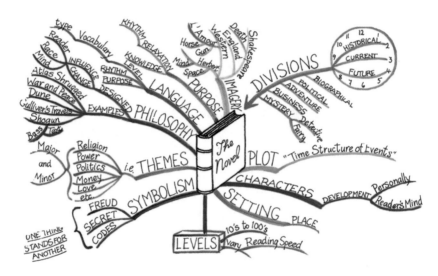

Mind Map by a father, Sean Adam, helping his daughter to pass her literature exams (which she did!)

Mind mapping notes from a lecture

In order to make your note-taking task easier, you could ask the lecturer or speaker beforehand if they will give you a summary of the major topics, themes or categories that are to be dealt with in the session. If this is not possible, simply construct a Mind Map while listening, searching for basic ordering ideas as the lecture progresses. After the lecture you can edit, re-order and refine your Mind Map, a process which will force you to make sense of the information, preparation and presentation, thus enhancing comprehension and memory of it. You can also use templates to facilitate your note-taking. Add the key words of your template on to the main branches of your Mind Map. For example, the 'six Ws' (Who, What, Where, Why, When, How), or SWOT (Strengths, Weaknesses, Opportunities, Threats), or Edward de Bono's PNI (Positive, Negative, Interesting).

Use words and pictures, and jump around

Note down the incoming information using words and pictures. Jump from one branch to another if needed. If you are a Mind Map beginner, you will sometimes notice that you write down far too much in phrases and sentences. Do not worry about this. You will quickly make progress and note less and less because you will realise, little by little, that with only a few key words, your amazing brain will be able to retrieve all the information. This way you will have more time to participate and engage 'intelligently' in meetings and discussions.

Don't censor your brain

If an idea that pops up seems irrelevant to you, put it as a secondary idea on a branch without any basic ordering idea. Keep doing this for every apparently 'irrelevant' idea that your brain gives you. In the end, your brain will give meaning to this branch which very often results in 'aha!' moments.

Make it memorable

The flow of information is sometimes so fast that you will not have enough time even to change coloured pens. Again, do not worry about this. Use a single colour if you have to; however, if you want to remember the information from your Mind Map, adding colours and drawings will help your brain in leaps and bounds. Take a couple of minutes, within 24 hours of the session, to make your Mind Map memorable.

Create blanks

If you realise you have missed something, draw an empty main or second-level branch where you think you 'lost' something. At the end of the communication, these empty branches will 'blink' and they will allow you to ask questions to fill them in.

Add on

It may happen that you reach the border of the page while the information flow on that particular branch in your Mind Map keeps going. In that case simply add a new page to your Mind Map and stick it to the starting page later on, or commence a new Mind Map, coding from which key word/area it emanates. This situation will only arise in hand-drawn Mind Maps. Computer Mind Maps will allow you to mind map to infinity!

Overcoming obstacles

Many people find it difficult to take notes during a meeting, lecture or training course. If the information to be noted is well structured, it is not too painful, but in reality information 'senders' tend to jump from one subject to another. When the information 'sender' gets carried away by their own associative thought processes, the question for the note-taker becomes, 'What should I write down?' 'Where should I put that piece of information?' and the flow of ideas coming through is blocked. With a Mind Map, if the speaker jumps from one subject to another, the Mind Mapper can also freely jump from one 'branch' to another with the speaker. So a Mind Map is the ideal tool for 'capturing' and managing those thoughts. Moreover, keeping to one single page of paper (as opposed to sheets of paper with linear note-taking) allows a better overview. Because it utilises support images and single key words, a Mind Map makes it easier to see the connections between different items, and gives you both a micro and a macro view.

Take a moment to review the Mind Map on the next page, which is a summary of getting the most from note-taking with Mind Maps. Once you have tried Mind Maps a few times you'll realise just how limiting linear notes are, and just how enjoyable, liberating and productive Mind Map notes are.

Now you've completed your first bold step into Mind Map applications, it's time to broaden things and look at how Mind Maps can benefit all aspects of your life.

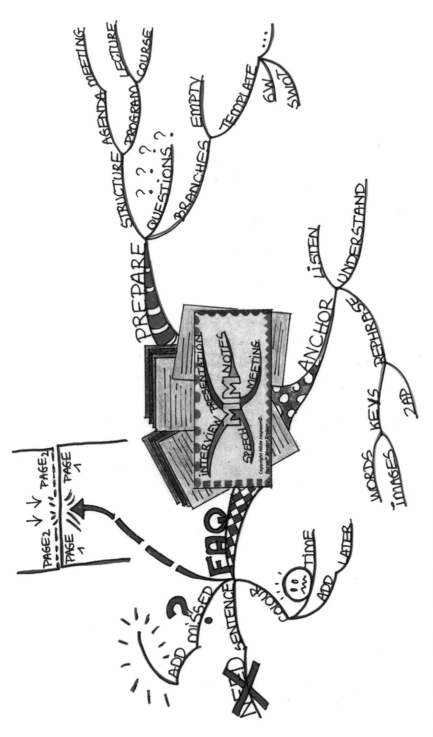

How to get the most from note-taking with Mind Maps

'Mind-mapping' software **can also be used** as a digital 'blank slate' to help **connect and synthesize ideas and data** – and ultimately **create new knowledge** . . . and **mental models** to help people mine and assess the value of **all that information**.

Bill Gates, 'The Road Ahead: How "intelligent agents" and Mind Mappers are taking our information democracy to the next stage', *Newsweek*, 25 January 2006

Part 4
Mind Maps in study, life and work

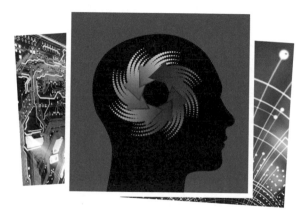

The beauty of Mind Maps is that they free up our thinking, opening us up to infinite possibilities of thought. Because they mirror our natural and radiant thought processes, you'll find that you don't want to stop – the more you mind map, the more you *want* to mind map.

In Part 4 you'll be introduced to the broader applications of the mind map in your study, work and life. Whether it's analysing issues, assessing goals, making plans, carrying out research, revising for an exam, speaking in public, managing a team – the list is infinite!

Mind Maps for self-analysis

This chapter explores how you can use Mind Maps to analyse your own life – whether it's to gain a greater insight into yourself, to set some immediate or long-term goals, Mind Maps are a powerful tool to take your life forward. You'll also learn how to use Mind Maps to help other people analyse their own lives, and we'll be looking at some fascinating examples of self-analysis Mind Maps.

Why use Mind Maps for self-analysis?

If you're weighing up the pros and cons of changing your job or trying to work out your long-term priorities, Mind Maps can be an enormous help in clarifying your thoughts and feelings.

Because Mind Maps give you both a big-picture view *and* reveal the individual, they help you to identify trends in your life while giving you insight into specific things that you may or may not do. This allows you to explore one of the most complicated subjects – you – in an accessible way; it also enables you to stand back from your life and look at things objectively. Once you see your life 'mapped' out in this way, you are in an ideal position to spot problems and opportunities, and plan ahead for a happy and successful future.

How to use a Mind Map to get a 'complete picture'

It is helpful to begin with a 'complete-picture' self-analysis Mind Map. There are three stages to this.

1 Quick-fire Mind Map burst

Draw a central image which captures either your physical or your conceptual idea of yourself or the situation. Then do a quick-fire Mind Map burst, allowing a full and free flow of facts, thoughts and emotions. Make sure you do this quickly – working at speed will make it easier to express all your ideas and stop you censoring yourself.

2 Reconstruction and revision

Before you start on the next stage, take a short break to relax your brain. When you return, select your basic ordering ideas. These could be: personal history (past, present and future); strengths; weaknesses; likes; dislikes; emotions; hobbies; achievements; work; long-term goals; short-term goals; responsibilities; friends; family; partner.

Having completed your quick-fire Mind Map burst and selected your major branches, you should create a larger, more artistic and more considered version. This final Mind Map is the external mirror of your internal state.

3 Reflection

After you've completed your final Mind Map, take some time to look over it and weigh up your findings. You are essentially holding your life in your hands – it's a powerful perspective. You'll notice patterns, things that excited you, things that didn't. It might be that this Mind Map is enough, and you can make some decisions from looking at this, but it may be that you need to create more quick-fire Mind Maps to reach clarity. Take as much time as you need and add to this 'complete-picture' Mind Map as things emerge.

Yong Sheng's story

My name is Yong Sheng and I am from Singapore. I have been an avid Mind Mapper since I first picked up one of Tony's books when I was 14. I am currently in my second year at Loughborough University studying Sports Science with Management.

I met Tony Buzan when he came to Singapore for his seminars and contacted him on a regular basis with updates about my progress in pursuing my dream of becoming an Olympic champion in the decathlon. This Mind Map is one of my monthly Mind Map progress reports to Tony.

The branch 'Events' is used to quickly summarise my current state on the different events and how I am faring. The 'Strategy' branch is my current thinking and planning

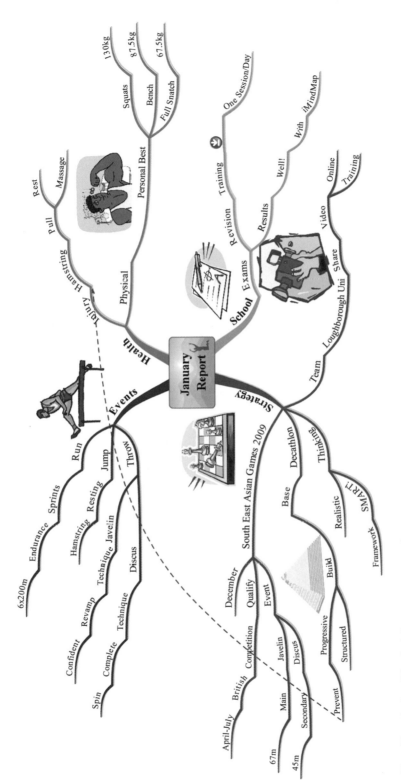

Yong Sheng's decathlon training progress report

on how to proceed. The Health' branch summarises the current state that my body is in, and the 'School' branch looks at the school events that may affect me.

What I didn't realise is how good a snapshot it provides me of how I was in January. When I review it, I feel like 'wow' – I didn't realise I progressed that much since January! However I am not yet at an elite level, and when I started pursuing this dream of becoming a decathlete, I was nowhere near fit enough, with a knee injury I picked up during the army, or performing at a level that would seem plausible to win the Olympic medal in one of the hardest events of all, decathlon.

This May I performed quite badly in the UK competitions that I took part in and once again it is very frustrating, plus my injury didn't seem to be holding up well. Thus I will be missing the South East Asian Games 2009 as stated in my strategy branch. So the past few months have not been easy. I worked hard to iron out my weaknesses, and now looking back at my personal best for gym exercises in January, I made significant process. I guess now all I have to do is to mind map out a better plan, and continue pushing ahead.

Past and future goals

An annual personal review of past achievements and projection of future goals is extremely useful in ordering and planning your life, and the Mind Map is the ideal tool for both these tasks.

Having completed a review of your current situation as a 'complete-picture' Mind Map, you can use the same Mind Map as the basis for another Mind Map describing your plan of action for the coming year. In this way you can use the next year to build on your current strengths and priorities, and perhaps choose to spend less time and energy on areas which have proved less productive or satisfying in the past.

As the years go by, these annual Mind Maps form an ongoing record, revealing trends and patterns over your whole lifetime and giving you major insights into yourself and the path your life is taking.

As well as annual Mind Maps, you should do a 'complete-picture' Mind Map at the beginning and end of any important phase in your life, whether you are changing job or house, or beginning or ending a relationship or course of study.

Helping others to analyse themselves

You may wish to help friends or colleagues analyse themselves, perhaps someone who has never done a Mind Map before. To do this, use a 'complete-picture' Mind Map, the only difference being that, rather than analysing yourself, you become a scribe and guide for someone else.

Your friends or colleagues can describe their central images while you draw them. They can then dictate all the thoughts, feelings and ideas that come to mind, while you write them down as a quick-fire Mind Map burst. You will need to help them find suitable basic ordering ideas and draw a comprehensive Mind Map incorporating everything that they have said. When you have completed this, you can then analyse the Mind Map together.

Self-analysis Mind Maps

The Mind Map below is by a chief executive in a multinational corporation who originally wished to analyse his life in relation to his business activities. However, as the Mind Map increasingly revealed his feelings, it began to reflect all the major elements in his life. These included family, business, sporting activities, learning and general self-development, as well as his interest in Eastern philosophies and practices.

He subsequently explained that, before the mind mapping self-analysis, he had assumed his business to be his prime concern. But, with the help of his Mind Map, he realised that his family was the true foundation of his life. As a result, he transformed his relationship with his wife, children and other relatives, and adjusted his schedule to reflect his true priorities.

Predictably enough, his health and his mental state improved enormously, his family became much closer and more loving and his business improved dramatically as it began to reflect his new positive outlook.

Mind Map by a male CEO of a multinational organisation reconsidering his life and refocusing on his family

The Mind Map below was created by a female executive who was considering a change of career and personal direction. She did the Mind Map in order to see who she was and what her belief systems were. Initially she suffered from relatively low self-esteem. However, by the time she had completed her self-analysis, she was as radiant as the Mind Map itself.

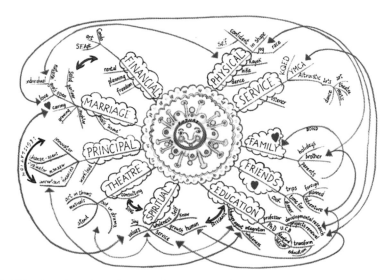

Mind Map by a female senior executive examining her belief system, herself and her chosen directions for the future

Mind Maps for a work–life balance

Mind Maps help you gain balance in life because they give you such an immediate perspective on where things are unbalanced. You can quickly mind map this using 'balance' as the central image, and then using the following main subject branches: health, family and friends, leisure, wealth, relationships, career/business and spiritual.

The following Mind Maps are examples of how a Mind Map can be used to map out work–life balance and personal/career goal setting.

Mikiko Chikada Kawase, who created the the Mind Map on page 125, says:

The Mind Map is filed in my day planner with other important Mind Maps (vision, mission and so on) so that I can frequently refer to it. This helps me not to lose sight of my life goals even during the very hectic hours and days. I started Mind Mapping for survival (or efficiency) almost 25 years ago. As a long-time Mind Mapper, I strongly believe that the benefit of using Mind Maps far exceeds my initial success at school.

Life balance Mind Map created by Mikiko Chikada Kawase

The Mind Map on page 127, is an example of setting goals using Buzan's iMindMap software. This Mind Map template provides a natural visual representation of goals. In both instances, the Mind Maps 'catch' whatever thoughts spring to mind in relation to setting personal goals and achieving a work–life balance. They allow the sequence of thoughts in the Mind Mapper's head to flow naturally and to be placed wherever they fit best on the Mind Map. Since association is rarely linear, the normal progression will involve quite a bit of leaping about from one branch to another as the sequence of thoughts dictates.

Mind Maps for personal problem-solving

You can use Mind Maps both to solve personal problems and to resolve difficulties in your relationships with others. The skills you have already acquired in self-analysis and decision-making (see Chapter 12) play a major part in problem-solving.

The process of using Mind Maps for personal problem-solving is almost identical to self-analysis except that the focus is on a specific personality trait or characteristic that may be causing you concern. For example, imagine that your problem is excessive shyness. You begin with a central image (perhaps a picture of you hiding your face behind your hands), then do a quick-fire Mind Map burst, releasing all the thoughts and emotions triggered by the idea of shyness.

In the first reconstruction and revision, your basic ordering ideas might include:

● The situations in which you feel shy.

● The emotions which constitute your shyness.

● The physical reactions you experience.

● The verbal and physical behaviour that results.

● The background to your shyness (when it first started and how it developed) and the possible root causes.

Having comprehensively defined, analysed and incubated the problem, you need to do a second reconstruction and revision. In this second Mind Map you should look at each element of the problem and work out a specific plan of action to solve it. Implementing these various actions should then enable you to resolve the problem in its entirety.

In some cases it may turn out that you are mistaken about the real problem. If the same word or concept appears on several branches, the chances are that it is actually more fundamental to your problem than the one you have placed in the centre. In this situation you should simply start another Mind Map, with the new key concept as your central image, and continue as before.

In addition to self-analysis and problem-solving, Mind Maps can play many other useful roles in everyday life. In the next chapter we find out how to use a Mind Map diary – the ultimate organiser.

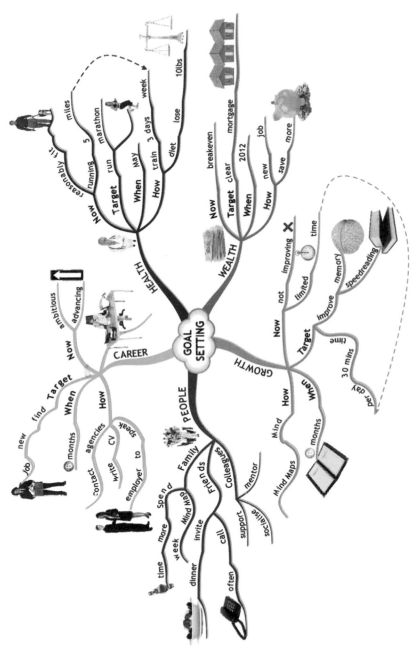

Goal-setting Mind Map using Buzan's iMindMap software

The Mind Map diary

Traditional diaries and organisers place us firmly under the tyranny of linear time. In this chapter you will be introduced to a new, revolutionary Mind Map diary which allows you to manage your time according to your needs and desires rather than the other way round. The Mind Map diary can be used both as a forward planning diary and as a retrospective record of events, thoughts and feelings.

As you work your way through this chapter, you may find it useful to visit www.imindmap.com/resources to log on and download an iMindMap diary template, to help you get started with your own Mind Map diary.

Why keep a diary/organiser with Mind Maps?

The Mind Map diary is visually attractive, unlike traditional diaries, and becomes more attractive as the Mind Mapper's skills improve. If you don't enjoy planning and organising your life, the Mind Map diary will help you get over this as it is so visually stimulating – it actually encourages you to use it. This differs greatly from standard diaries, which many people subconsciously reject – 'forgetting' to put things in their diaries, putting them in the wrong place or feeling guilty about not using them at all.

The Mind Map diary's use of image, colour-coding and branching associations gives you instant access to the information, providing both a macroscopic and a microscopic view of your life: effectively a life-management tool. It allows you to span future and past; to plan and record.

The Mind Map diary is an externalised memory-core of your life and puts every event in the context of your whole life. Reviewing your diary becomes almost like 'going to the movies' of your life!

The principles of the Mind Map diary

The yearly plan

The yearly plan gives an overview of the major events in the year. On the next page is an iMindMap example showing a wedding plan – a major event that requires diary planning over a long period. As with any Mind Map, start with a central image (this one mimics a wedding invitation). The basic ordering ideas are the 12 months of the year. Each month has one or two major sub-branches (i.e. March's is 'invitations', April's is 'service' and August's is 'outfits'). From these sub-branches more branches naturally emanate, such as 'accommodation', 'location' and 'cost' for 'honeymoon' and so on.

The obvious benefit of mind mapping your year in this way is that it gives you an instant snapshot of what's ahead and is quickly understood by other people – so perfect to plan something that requires collaboration, such as a wedding.

I use my annual Mind Map as an 'anno planner'. I record the major events of each month using basic ordering ideas, colour coding, symbols and images. At the end of that year I mind map the year that has just passed and the year that is about to commence. For future planning I copy the major elements from the previous year, making sure, at a glance, that I am 'balanced' in terms of the amount of time spent writing, travelling, lecturing, consulting, creating new books, and time spent with myself . At the end of the process I have a beautiful overview of the year and its spatial activity–rest rhythm. Having masterminded this by Mind Map, I can drill down into a monthly breakdown and use that as a basis for the daily diary (see example on page 132).

Observe how the Mind Map planner makes extensive use of colours, symbols and images to make key milestones stand out. You should establish your own colour codes to give secrecy where necessary. With consistent colour coding, it is possible to get an instant overview of the whole of the coming year. This colour coding should be continued in your monthly and daily plans, to give consistency and immediacy in cross-referencing, planning and recall.

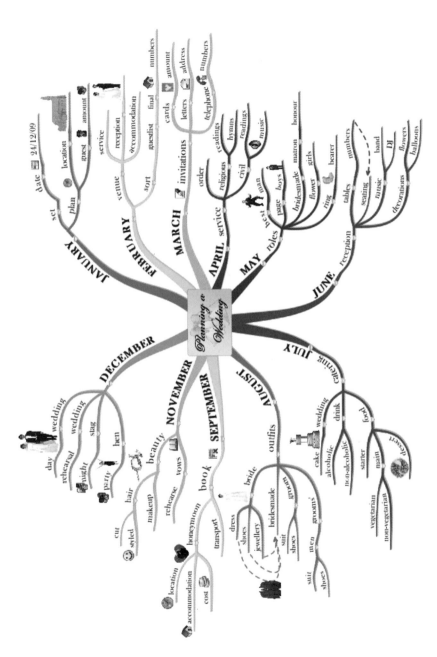

iMindMap wedding plan designed for a year long planning

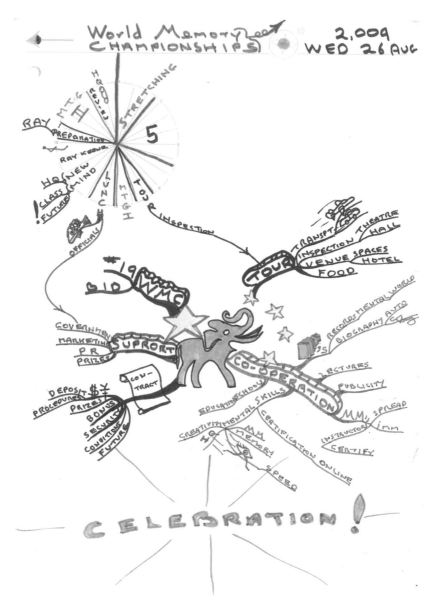

This is a Mind Map done by Tony Buzan as a diary entry. The 24-hour clock logs the key elements of the day. The Mind Map summarises an all-day meeting in Guangzhou, China, in 2009, to discuss the Chinese bid to host the 19th World Memory Championships in Guangzhou. The central image incorporates the World Memory Championships symbol, the Memory Elephant, and the five stars of the Chinese flag. The Mind Map diary entry summarises the tour of inspection, the areas of co-operation offered by the bidders, the support systems, and the main elements of the contract. Subsequent to the meeting, and after consideration by the World Memory Sports Council, Guangzhou was declared the winning city for the 2010 World Memory Championships.

The monthly plan

The monthly Mind Map diary is an expanded version of the single month from the yearly plan. Look at the iMindMap on page 134 to see how this is done.

The Mind Mapper has started from the '2 o'clock' position (but you can start at any point) of the main branches, being your four weeks. The sub-branches in this example are 'set aside days' of the week to accomplish the many tasks (and it is amazing how many interlinked tasks are needed) to ensure a successful, stress-free holiday. Key words, colour, images and symbols heighten the imagination and association process needed to stimulate both recall and what to do next.

The weekly plan

On page 136 is a weekly Mind Map diary for a seven-day fitness regime. It starts with a central image (which is preferable for triggering associated processes in the brain). The main branches – in this example the seven days of the week again start from '2 o'clock' (but that option is up to you) with Monday – are made thicker than the secondary branches, which in this example are consistently set as 'diet', 'exercise' and 'rest' – the key considerations for a fitness regime. Colour, images and symbols will boost commitment both to the regime and to the diary.

The daily plan

The daily Mind Map diary page is based on the 24-hour clock. As with the yearly and monthly plans, the Mind Map laws are applied. At the end of the day you can monitor your progression by adding 'ticks' to those items accomplished, thus giving you a greater sense of achievement.

In the simple iMindMap on page 137, five thick main branches – 'morning', 'lunch', 'afternoon', 'evening', 'miscellaneous' – radiate from a central theme, but you can choose your own key words and themes. Colour, images and symbols help to break up the various periods and activities. Like the yearly and monthly plans, these daily plans can be used to review any period in your life, either comprehensively or in depth. A quick browse can bring back a whole week, month or year with glorious vividness.

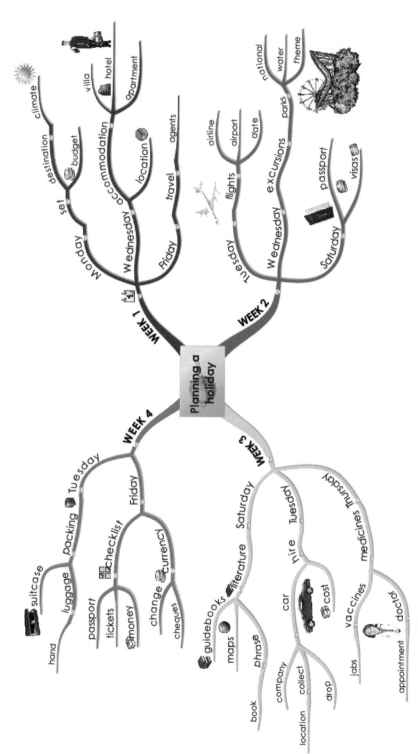

Example of a monthly Mind Map diary – planning a holiday

A daily diary can work on the premise that the day is 24 hours (whereas standard diaries tend to go by daylight hours only). On the top left-hand side you could put a 24-hour clock (see the example on page 138). In that clock you can colour code and create images for the main elements of your day – at their appropriate time slots. This is the 'vision statement' – for example, what it is you want to achieve that day. Then, at the start of the day, you can add your main Mind Map, which is the essence of that day – an important meeting, for instance. The diary page then becomes a record of what you did that day and acts as a specific record of such things as meetings.

The Mind Map diary takes advantage of the 'whole-picture' view that Mind Maps offer, as well as the combination of dimension and gestalt (the 'completing tendency') which make them even more beneficial because there is a natural stimulation to work through the diary tasks.

Yearly and monthly plans provide the ideal basis for your annual review of the past and for the setting of future goals. Cross-referencing, calculation and observation of overall trends all become much easier when you have an overview of the whole year.

In the next chapter, on study skills, you'll find just how useful this 'snap-shot' perspective is when it comes to studying and revising.

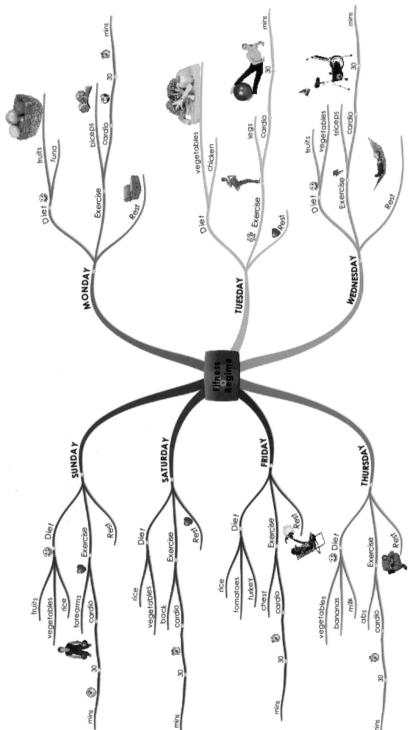

Example of a weekly Mind Map diary – fitness regime

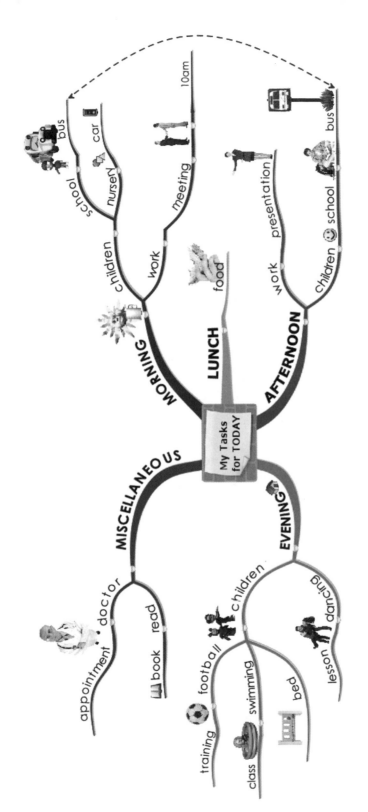

Example of an iMindMap day planner

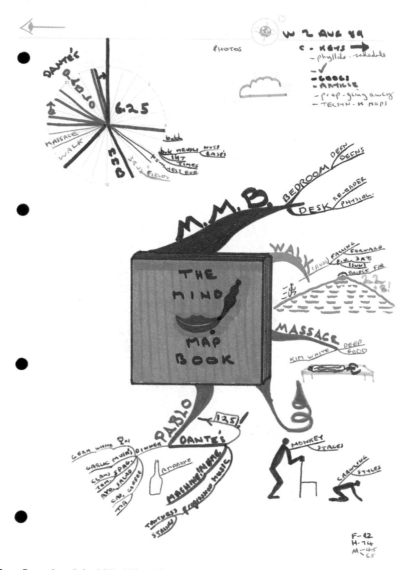

Tony Buzan's original Mind Map diary – the diary Mind Map of the birth of The Mind Map Book

Mind Maps for study skills

In this chapter you'll find out how Mind Maps can completely transform your relationship to study – and the results and satisfaction you get from it. You'll find out how to apply Mind Maps to four major study areas – writing essays, taking exams, completing projects or reports, and how to mind map larger pieces of information – and how this will help you learn and achieve more than you'd ever imagined possible.

Why use Mind Maps for study skills?

Because Mind Maps fit so much on one page, they massively reduce the time needed to prepare and structure work, giving you a whole-picture view at all times. And because everything is so accessible – you're not dealing with pages and pages of notes – they eliminate the stress and unhappiness caused by disorganisation and feeling overwhelmed. Their unique, colourful and creative designs bring to life something that, in linear note form, seemed so boring and 'heavy'. This is enhanced by the fact that Mind Maps allow you to relate your own thoughts and ideas to those expressed in a book or lecture, engaging and motivating you directly. The effect of all this is to totally revolutionise your approach to study.

How to mind map an essay

If you are planning to take an exam where you have to write essays under pressure, once you get to grips with the method below, try giving yourself a set amount of time in which to complete it so you have practised working under time pressure.

1 Begin your Mind Map with a central image, representing the subject of your essay.

2 Draw you basic ordering ideas from this subject, paying close attention to the question that you are answering and the topics you need to cover to achieve this.

3 Now let your mind range freely, adding items of information, or points you wish to make, wherever they seem most relevant on your Mind Map. There is no limit to the number of branches and sub-branches that can radiate outwards. Use colours, symbols, or both, to indicate cross-referencing or association between different areas.

4 Next, edit and reorder your Mind Map into a cohesive whole.

5 Now sit down and write the first draft of your essay, using the Mind Map as a framework. A well-organised Mind Map should provide you with all the main subdivisions of the essay, the key points to be mentioned in each and the way in which those points relate to each other. At this stage you should write as quickly as possible, skipping over any areas that cause you special difficulty, especially particular words or grammatical structures. In this way you will create a much greater flow, and you can always return to the 'problem areas' later, much as you would when studying a reference book.

6 If you come up against 'writer's block', doing another Mind Map will help you overcome it. In many cases just drawing the central image will get your mind going again, playing and freewheeling round the topic of your essay. If you get blocked once more, simply add new sub-branches from the main branches and key words and images you have so far generated, and your brain's natural gestalt or 'completing tendency' will fill in the blank spaces with new words and images.

7 Finally, review your Mind Map and put the finishing touches to your essay, adding cross-references, supporting your argument with more evidence or quotations, and modifying or expanding your conclusions where necessary.

The Mind Map produced from these guidelines is supposed to replace the pages of notes that most students write before actually writing their essays. The Mind Map method uses a single Mind Map in place of the standard 20 pages of notes, not to mention the numerous drafts.

> Use a Mind Map – save a tree
> Use Mind Maps – save a forest

Have a look at the following three Mind Maps to see how they helped students write essays on sport, Sweden and computers.

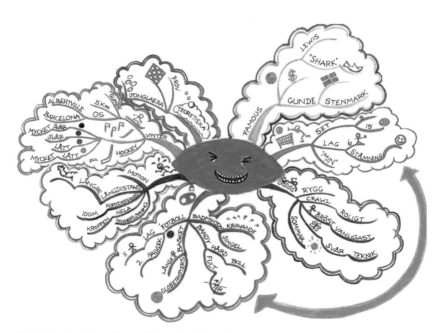

Mind Map by Karen Schmidt on school sports

Mind Map by Katarina Naiman for a school project on Sweden

To give you an idea of how powerful Mind Maps can be to the essay process, after completing her essay, one of the students said: 'The more I wrote and drew, the more things came to my mind – the more ideas I got, the more brave and original they were – Mind Maps are never ending!

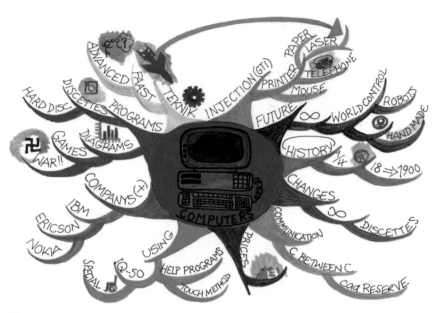

Mind Map by Thomas Enskog for a school project on computers

How to mind map for an exam

1   The first step is to read the examination paper fully, selecting the questions you plan to answer and noting, in a mini Mind Map, any thoughts that immediately spring to mind on reading the questions.

2   Next, you have to decide in what order you are going to answer the questions and how much time you will devote to each.

3   Resist the temptation to start answering the first question in detail straight away, and do quick-fire Mind Map bursts on all the questions you intend to answer. By following this procedure, you enable your mind to explore, throughout the examination, the ramifications of all the questions, regardless of the particular question you are answering at any given time.

4   Now go back to your first question and do a Mind Map to act as the framework for your answer. The central image corresponds to your introductory comments, while each of the major branches provides a major subheading or section of the essay. For each extension from your major branches you should be able to write a paragraph or two.

5   As you build up your answer, you will find that you can begin to cross-refer throughout your knowledge structure, and can conclude by adding your own thoughts, associations and interpretations. Such an answer will demonstrate to the examiner a comprehensive knowledge, an ability to

analyse, organise, integrate and cross-refer, and especially an ability to come up with your own creative and original ideas on the subject. In other words, you will have achieved top marks!

The following Mind Map is one that student James Lee created for a History exam, outlining the main explanations given for the commencement of the Second World War. It is one of hundreds of Mind Maps James has done. He prepared these Mind Maps to help him pass his senior and university entrance examinations. At the age of 15 James missed six months of schooling because of illness and was advised to go back a year in view of the fact that his GCSE examinations loomed on the horizon. James persuaded his teachers to let him 'go for it' and started to mind map everything in sight! In just three months he did a year's work, and in ten examinations scored seven As and three Bs.

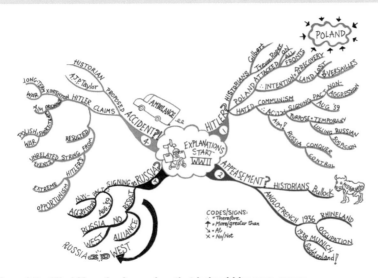

One of the Mind Maps by James Lee that helped him pass exams

How to mind map projects and reports

Writing a project or report, ranging from a few pages to the length of a doctoral thesis, can be made much easier by using Mind Maps. Such projects may involve extensive research and final presentation in written, graphic and oral form, but the approach is essentially the same as that used for essays and examinations.

As in any study task, the first step is deciding how much you plan to cover within a given time. These time–volume targets are just as important in long-term projects as in short-term ones. Then, during the research phase, you can use Mind Maps to take notes from source material, to write up research results, to organise and integrate your ideas as they emerge, and to form the basis of your final written or oral presentation. As with mind mapping an essay or examination answer, projects and reports written in this way are likely to be much better structured, and more focused, creative and original, than those based on the laborious traditional methods of linear note-taking, drafting and re-drafting.

How to memorise a book with a Mind Map

Mind mapping a book for study will save you writing pages and pages of notes. You can either mind map the book as you read, or mark the book while reading and complete your Mind Map afterwards.

Here's an example of how you might tap in to a Mind Map to improve your memory phenomenally.

On the next page you will find a Mind Map by John Naisbitt, the futurist and author of *Megatrends* and *Megatrends 2000*. His book predicted ten major trends for the nineties and noughties. Whilst I briefly explain each major trend in the text below, refer to the relevant branch on the Mind Map.

Trend 1: The economy will become increasingly information based, and 'learning how to learn' is what it really is all about. The only people who will be 'left behind' will be those who remain rigid and linear in their thinking.

Trend 2: There will be a renaissance in the arts, literature and spirituality. Attendance in courses on these subjects is up all around the world. People are seeking to get in touch with themselves more and find a balance between nature and technology.

Trend 3: The cities will decline. They will decline as the essential centres of all commerce and trade. Because of the growth of electronic commerce, all transportation will decrease and we will no longer need lorries and trucks transporting goods. Also, buildings are becoming 'intelligent' and therefore we do not need to travel into the cities to transact intelligent operations.

Trend 4: Socialism, in the form of state welfare, will 'rest in peace', and capitalism and democracy will become the world's major economic and political systems.

Trend 5: English will become the global language – the majority of people will learn English either as their primary or secondary language. 80 per cent of science and technology language and terms are spoken in English.

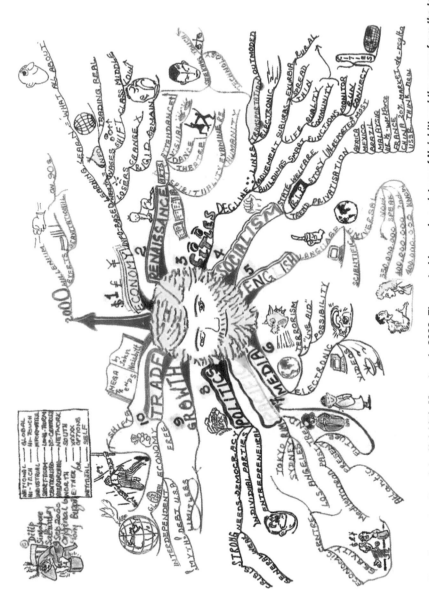

A Mind Map created by Tony Buzan of author John Naisbitt and the arrow from the top of his head represents his vision of the future. The ten numbered branches correspond to the ten major areas of change predicted by Naisbitt over this time span.

Trend 6: Media will become increasingly global and electronic, and every electronic device will have the capability of connecting with every other device. The world will become a 'global brain'.

Trend 7: The Pacific Rim, including the west coast of America and the east coast of Asia, as well as Australia, will become the prime centre of gravity for the economy, business and trade.

Trend 8: Politics will become more entrepreneurial and more and more people will gain the 'capital', not only of money, but also the 'capital' of media and communicative ability. Naisbitt predicts that there will be far more individual causes with their own particular focuses.

Trend 9: Growth will become limitless. Naisbitt predicts this because of its link with the first megatrend – the economy becoming information based. The potential for the generation of the human brain is infinite.

Trend 10: Trade will become free and, like many of the other megatrends, global. Because of the combination of these trends, Naisbitt predicts the world will become more peaceful, as symbolised by the little dove above the Earth.

When you've finished reading, I want you to close the book, and see how much of the *Mind Map* you can remember by roughly sketching your own Mind Map.

That was a 400-page book! You have 'read' it in less than three minutes and have a unique recollection of it, your Mind Map. Use this Mind Map as a memory trigger for the book – you'll be pleasantly surprised at just how much you remember.

Mind mapping while you read is like having an ongoing 'conversation' with the author, reflecting your developing pattern of knowledge as the book progresses. The growing Mind Map also enables you to keep checking your level of understanding and adjusting the focus of your information-gathering.

Mind mapping afterwards means that you produce your Mind Map having gained a complete understanding of the book's content and the way each part relates to the others. Your Mind Map will therefore be more comprehensive and focused, and less likely to require revision.

Whichever method you choose, it is important to remember that mind mapping a book is a two-way process. The aim is not simply to duplicate the author's thoughts in Mind Map form. Rather, it is a question of organising and integrating the author's thoughts in the context of your own knowledge, understanding, interpretation and specific goals. Your Mind Map should include your own comments, thoughts and creative realisations arising from what you have read. Using different colours or codes will enable you to distinguish your own contributions from those of the author.

The technique for this has already been described in Chapter 13 (see page 111) – here's a quick recap:

1 Browse.

2 Set time and targets.

3 Make a Mind Map of existing knowledge on the subject.

4 Define aims and objectives.

5 Overview and draw the central image and main branches.

6 Preview – what you didn't see in the overview. Add to the Mind Map.

7 Inview – identify issues and leave any problems out. Add to the Mind Map.

8 Review – go over any skipped areas and problems, and complete the Mind Map.

How to mind map a lecture/presentation/film

Mind Maps are perfect for recording 'live' information, as speakers often jump around topics and repeat things. Mind Maps allow you to mirror this process, unlike linear notes. See Chapter 13 for an explanation of this technique.

Creating a master Mind Map

If you are involved in a long-term course of study it is a good idea to keep a giant master Mind Map, reflecting the major subdivisions, themes, theories, personalities and events within that subject. Every time you read a book or go to a lecture, you can record any major new insight on your master Mind Map, thus creating an external mirror-image of your growing network of internal knowledge.

Those who have done mind mapping of this kind notice a surprising and rewarding trend. After a reasonable length of time, the boundaries of their Mind Maps begin to edge into other subjects and disciplines. Thus the periphery of a master Mind Map on psychology begins to touch on neurophysiology, mathematics, philosophy, astronomy, geography, meteorology, ecology and so on.

This does not mean that your knowledge structure is disintegrating and moving too far from the point. It actually means that your knowledge is becoming so deep and extensive that it is beginning to relate to other areas of knowledge. This is the stage of intellectual development familiar to the great thinkers of history, in which all disciplines are found to relate to all others. It is also the stage at which your master Mind Map helps you to contribute to the continuing expansion of human knowledge.

Reviewing your Mind Maps

You should review your Mind Maps regularly in order to maintain your understanding and recall of what you have learnt. Rather than just looking at your original Mind Map for each review, it is best to start by doing another quick-fire Mind Map burst of what you remember. This will show what you are able to recall without any assistance. You can then check against your original Mind Map, adjusting any discrepancies and strengthening any areas of weak recall.

From mind mapping your own life to using Mind Maps to study, we now move on to Mind Maps in the business and professional environment. The next three chapters explain how to make your working life more organised, more productive and, not least, more rewarding and enjoyable.

Mind Maps for meetings

Applying Mind Maps in the workplace and boardroom brings enormous benefits (and I have devoted a whole new book to it in *Mind Maps for Business*). In the next few chapters we look at some key areas – meetings, presentations and management issues – where mind maps can make your working life easier, more enjoyable and more productive.

Why use Mind Maps in meetings?

The major applications of group Mind Maps include joint creativity, combined recall, group problem-solving and analysis, group decision-making, group project management, group training and education, and team building.

At meetings everyone should ideally be both a contributor and a member of the audience. Throughout the group mind mapping process, there is equal and consistent emphasis on individual and group input. The Mind Map becomes a vehicle for the individual to engage with their own mental universes, which is then used to feed back to the group. In this way, the group mind benefits from individual contributions *and* collective engagement.

Group mind mapping automatically creates an emerging consensus, building team spirit and focusing all minds on the group's goals and objectives. It also acts as hard copy for the group memory, and guarantees that at the end of the meeting each member of the group has a similar and comprehensive understanding of what has been achieved.

How to mind map on your own in a meeting

The subject of the meeting provides the central image, and the major items on the agenda correspond to the main branches. As the meeting progresses, you can add ideas and information wherever they seem most relevant. Alternatively, you may wish to have a mini Mind Map for each speaker. As long as these are all on the same large sheet of paper, it will be quite easy to indicate cross-references as themes and trends begin to emerge.

How to mind map a small meeting (two people)

The most basic Mind Map you can create in a meeting is between two people. To do this:

- Define the meeting subject/issue together.

- Complete a quick-fire Mind Map, individually.

- Come back together to discuss and exchange ideas.

- Create a joint Mind Map.

- Take a break to incubate the newly integrated ideas.

- Come back and revise the joint Mind Map.

- Analyse and make decisions.

In long-term projects (like the writing of this book) joint mind mapping has several advantages. The Mind Maps can be used as a way of ordering, recording and stimulating conversation in the many meetings that such a project requires. Using Mind Maps also enables you to conduct the process over a long time, and in numerous sessions, with continuity and momentum.

How to mind map as a group in a meeting

Group Mind Maps offer exciting possibilities in which groups of individuals can combine and multiply their personal creative abilities. The advantages of bringing individuals together in mind mapping groups was neatly summarised by Michael Bloch of the Sperry Laboratory:

In our daily lives, we learn a myriad of information that is unique to each of us. Because of this uniqueness, each of us has knowledge and a perspective that is strictly ours. Therefore it is beneficial to work with others during problem-solving tasks. By combining our Mind Map knowledge with others, we further the associations that we as well as others make.

During group brainstorming, the Mind Map becomes the external reflection of the group thinking, or the 'hard copy' of the group's memory. Throughout this process, individual brains combine their energy to create a separate 'group brain'. The Mind Map simultaneously reflects the evolution of this. At its best, it is impossible to distinguish the group Mind Map from one produced by a single great thinker.

To create a group Mind Map, you'll need to follow the preparation and application stages detailed in Chapter 16, along with these seven major stages:

1 Defining the subject

The topic is clearly and concisely defined, the objectives are set and the members of the group are given all the information that might be relevant to their deliberations.

2 Individual brainstorming

Each member of the group should spend at least one hour doing a quick-fire Mind Map burst and a reconstruction and revision Mind Map, showing major branches or basic ordering ideas – these are equivalent to stages 1 and 2 of the individual creative thinking mind mapping process in Chapter 11.

3 Small group discussion

The group now divides into smaller groups of three to five. In each group the members exchange their ideas and add to their own Mind Maps the ideas generated by other members. Allow one hour for this stage.

It is essential that a totally positive and accepting attitude be maintained. Whatever idea is mentioned by a group member should be supported and accepted by all the other members. In this way the brain which has generated the idea will be encouraged to continue exploring that chain of association. The next link in the chain may well turn out to be a profound insight, emanating from an idea that might have originally seemed weak, stupid or irrelevant.

4 Creation of first multiple-mind Mind Map

Having completed the small group discussion, the group is ready to create its first multiple-mind Mind Map.

A gigantic screen or wall-sized sheet of paper is used to record the basic structure. This can be done by the whole group, one good Mind Mapper from each small group or by one individual who acts as scribe for the whole group. Alternatively iMindMap can be used with a projector. Colour and form codes should be agreed on in order to ensure clarity of thought and focus.

Basic ordering ideas are selected for the main branches, and all ideas are incorporated in the Mind Map.

5 Incubation

It is essential to let the group Mind Map 'sink in', so a group break needs to be taken at this stage.

6 Second reconstruction and revision

After incubation, the group needs to repeat stages 2, 3 and 4 in order to capture the results of the newly considered and integrated thoughts. This means doing individual quick-fire Mind Map bursts, then producing reconstructed Mind Maps showing main branches, exchanging ideas, modifying the Mind Maps in small groups and, finally, creating a second group Mind Map. The two giant group Mind Maps can then be compared, in preparation for the final stage.

7 Analysis and decision-making

At this stage, the group uses the two Mind Maps to make critical decisions, set objectives and make plans.

The following Mind Map is a great example of a group Mind Map. It was created by a team of eight Digital executives working on the development of teamwork. Their conclusions were unremittingly positive!

Group mind mapping contrasts markedly with traditional brainstorming, in which one individual leads the group, noting in a list the key-word ideas given by other members on a flip chart or central screen. This is counter-productive because each word or concept publicly mentioned will create a gravitational pull that draws all members of the group in the same direction. In this way, traditional brainstorming groups negate the associative power of the individual brain, losing the massive gains that could be made by initially allowing each brain to explore its own uninterrupted thoughts on the topic.

Mind Maps in life, study and work

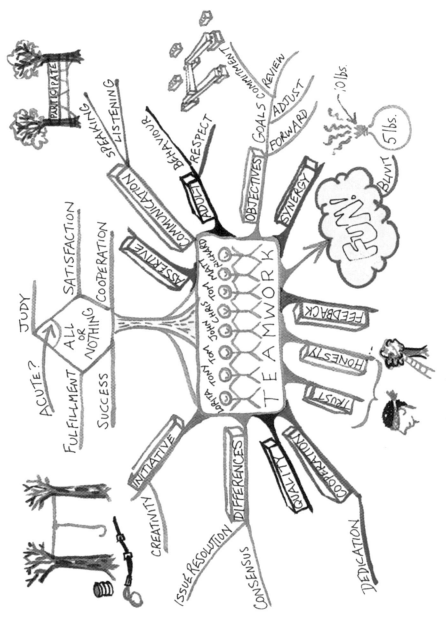

Mind Map on the development of teamwork by Digital executives

How to mind map larger meetings

For larger meetings, a master Mind Map can be created on a large board or chart that is visible to all, or projected on a screen using iMindMap. In this way the elected Mind Mapper can register every contribution and place it within the overall structure of the meeting. This avoids the all-too-common problem of good or brilliant ideas being discarded, or never emerging, because the traditional methods of structuring meetings and recording minutes counteract the growth of natural group communication. A group Mind Map can incorporate both brainstorming and planning.

A particular advantage of using Mind Maps in meetings is that the Mind Map gives a clearer and more balanced picture of the true content of the meeting. Research shows that in traditional meetings, preference is given either to those who speak first, last, loudest, with particular accents, with a higher level of vocabulary, or to those with a greater position of authority. The Mind Map cuts through this informational prejudice, gives a more objective and integrated view which allows everyone to be heard and encourages balanced participation and increased teamwork.

Chairing a meeting with a Mind Map

Mind Maps are particularly useful for chairing meetings. The chairperson has the agenda on a basic Mind Map and can use this fundamental frame to add thoughts, guide discussions and record the basic outline of what will eventually be the minutes of the meeting. Colour coding can be used to indicate action, ideas, question marks and important areas. Chairing a meeting this way allows the person in the chair to be much like a captain of a starship, guiding it safely through the clusters and galaxies of ideas.

A variation on this theme is to have a Mind Mapper sitting next to the chairman, in order to enable the chairman to participate on many levels at the same time, while keeping a constant overview of the developing thrust of the meeting.

By now you should start to see just how well Mind Maps fit into the work context and have a clear idea about how to use them collectively. The next major application for Mind Maps at work is in presentations – the focus of the next chapter.

Mind Maps for presentations

Presentations – whether on a one-to-one basis, in small or large groups, or via video conferencing – are a vital part of business life. Yet many of us are terrified of public speaking, more so than of spiders, snakes, diseases, war and even death! This chapter looks at how Mind Maps can help you present with impact, flair and clarity, so you'll never have to worry about or fear presentations again.

Why use Mind Maps for presentations?

Using a Mind Map, which only takes up a page, frees you to connect powerfully with your audience. You no longer have to worry about holding pages of notes and losing track of where you were. Without having to read a prepared speech, you allow yourself to speak naturally, to be yourself. You'll find that in this 'free' mode, all sorts of spontaneous things happen, keeping your audience interested and your energy at a high level.

Consider the presenter who had to make a speech at a three-day design conference in Washington DC, USA. The conference was attended by 2,300 delegates and our man was number 72 out of 75 speakers. He had to give his prepared speech from behind a podium and he was allotted the 'graveyard shift' – the slot that starts immediately after lunch. He was not a trained speaker, and as he approached the end of his 45-minute presentation most of the audience were dozing off. They all awoke at the alarmed conclusion of his speech, which was, 'Oh my God! The last page has gone!' The last page had indeed disappeared. And in that moment of sheer terror he had not the faintest idea what was on it!

Or take another presenter, who was an admiral presenting to a naval college. He tended to read his speeches in much the same way as an audio-typist transcribed it – perfectly but without any knowledge of its content. He was asked to give a speech to senior naval officials and, as he was short of time, he asked his aide to prepare a one-hour speech for him. He gave his presentation but began to suspect something was amiss when, after an hour, he found that he still had about the same number of pages to go.

Finally the truth dawned – he had been given two copies of the same speech. But the real horror was that the copies were ordered page 1, page 1, page 2, page 2, page 3, page 3, and so on. Because of his senior rank, no one had dared point out that perhaps this was carrying the mnemonic value of repetition a bit too far! A Mind Map would have saved him the embarrassment.

How to use Mind Maps to plan a presentation

Most presentations aren't as effective as they could be because people don't spend time preparing them. Sounds simple, but so many of us don't spend time on this crucial stage.

A presentation is essentially you communicating something to an audience. Before you can do this effectively, you need to be sure about who you are speaking to, what you want to say and how you need to say it to get the biggest impact. Most importantly, you'll find that spending time planning will leave you feeling confident and ready to speak – something you may never have thought possible!

Here's how you plan a presentation with a Mind Map:

1 Draw your central image that represents your presentation.

2 Do a quick-fire Mind Map burst of any ideas that come to mind which are in any way connected to the topic you have chosen.

3 Look again at your quick-fire Mind Map, create your main branches, your basic ordering ideas, and sub-branches, and fill in any other key words that come to mind. Each key word should take up at least one minute of your presentation, so it's a good idea to restrict your Mind Map to a maximum of 50 key words and images for a one-hour speech.

4 Look at your Mind Map again and pare it down even further, getting rid of all extraneous material. At this stage you should also put in codes to indicate where you wish to insert slides, videos, particular cross-references, examples and so on.

5 Now consider the order in which you wish to present your main branches and number them accordingly.

6 Finally, allocate an appropriate length of time to each branch, and then just follow your own instructions!

Freedom and flexibility – giving a Mind Map presentation

Use the Mind Map you created when planning your presentation. As Mind Maps are so visual, you don't necessarily need to hold the Mind Map – you'll be able to see your branches from somewhere nearby. You may also find it helpful to show the audience your Mind Map at the start, projected on a screen – you could refer back to it at various stages to clarify where you are. Mind Maps lend themselves ideally to this as they are so interesting, and often beautiful, to look at. You could also, to hold the audience's interest and ensure that they follow the pattern of thought, build up a Mind Map as your presentation progresses, introducing it as a 'simple little map of ideas'.

Unlike notes, it's easy to edit your Mind Map as the presentation goes on, so do keep it near you with pens at the ready. This is especially useful if the audience has particular needs or questions that arise, either before or during your speech – you can immediately link them into the Mind Map, making your presentation particularly relevant to your specific audience. Equally, if the time available for your presentation suddenly expands or shrinks, you can edit quickly and easily.

The flexibility of a Mind Map allows you to monitor your progress and to accelerate or expand your presentation accordingly. Perfectly timed performances are impressive in themselves, as well as courteous to other speakers and the audience.

If you are presenting with other speakers, you can quickly add to or alter your Mind Map, highlighting points for agreement, deleting any repetition. On the other hand, if the previous speaker has made misinformed or illogical comments, these can be linked into your Mind Map and then expanded in your presentation in order to encourage subsequent discussion and debate.

Example of a mind mapped presentation

Mind Maps have proved so useful in presentations that neuro-psychologist and author Michael J. Gelb has written an entire book, *Present Yourself*, based on the Mind Map approach.

The Mind Map shown on page 159 is a snapshot of the entire 114-page book *Present Yourself* by Michael Gelb with a foreword by Tony Buzan. It was created by world Mind Mapping Champion Phil Chambers. This explains how to give effective presentations in Mind Map form.

The Mind Map at the top of page 160 was prepared by Tony Buzan, for the Young Presidents' Organisation Faculty, as a welcoming speech given to an international body of professors and dignitaries (who were lecturing aboard the QE2 cruise liner). The Mind Map served as both the basis for the opening speech and a review for the participating faculty.

The third Mind Map is by Raymond Keene, OBE, Grandmaster in Chess, chess correspondent for *The Times* and *Spectator*, and the most prolific author on chess and thinking in the history of the field. The Mind Map was in preparation for a lecture Raymond Keene gave in Spanish on Spanish TV (*Television España* for the programme *En Jaque*). The Mind Map was on the great sixteenth-century Spanish chess player and writer Ruy Lopez and the intellectual and political influences of his time.

Keene said:

> *The virtue of a Mind Map when preparing a speech or writing an article is two-fold: the writer is constantly stimulated by the branching trees of ideas to new and more daring thoughts; while at the same time the key words and images ensure that in the verbiage of speaking and writing, no major point is overlooked.*
>
> *The Mind Map is particularly useful in this context. Without turning or shuffling any pages, it is possible to inform the audience in advance about the structure and key points. Because you are always operating from one sheet, you can tell your audience what you plan to say, you can say it with confidence and then you can recap to demonstrate you have proved your point. With linear notes, the danger is ending simply where the notes stop, in essence a random moment, often determined by chronology rather than meaning.*
>
> *Assuming that the lecturer has complete command of his or her subject, the key words act as a catalyst for enthusiasm and ex tempore ideas instead of a dry recitation of facts often determined by dates (i.e. lecture starts at the beginning of subject's life and finishes at the end) rather than significant content. If the lecturer does not have perfect grasp of the subject, linear notes simply make it worse. Whether writing an article or giving a verbal lecture, the Mind Map acts like a steering wheel to navigate through the main oceans of the presentation.*

Keene wrote this as part of an article for *The Times*; and it was based on the Mind Map he used for his presentation on Spanish television.

Having explored how to use Mind Maps in meetings and presentations, the next chapter broadens the focus to look at the way Mind Maps can be used to enhance communication and increase efficiency in management situations.

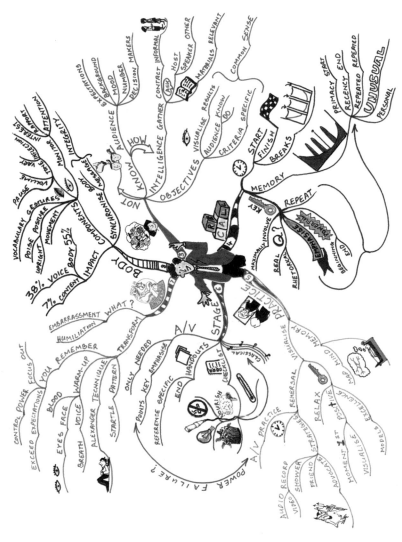

A Mind Map of Michael Gelb's entire book Present Yourself created by Phil Chambers

Mind Map by Tony Buzan for a welcoming speech

Mind Map by Raymond Keene OBE in preparation for a lecture given on Spanish television

Mind Maps for management

Mind Maps, because they provide both a complete picture and a view of all the individual parts, are the perfect tool for managers. In this chapter, we'll explore how Mind Maps can help managers increase team performance, implement strategy and help with overall communication and planning issues. We'll also look at specific case studies that illustrate this.

Why use Mind Maps for management?

One of the biggest problems in management is lack of clarity, lack of control and poor communication. Mind Maps overcome this by giving a big picture and small picture view simultaneously – so nothing is kept hidden. Mind Maps also allow for collaboration – the process of creating a collective Mind Map bonds teams together. Mind Maps are also so accessible – there's nothing more intimidating than scores of linear notes and graphs. Mind Maps, by their very nature, draw people in, make them feel included, part of a team.

How to use Mind Maps to improve teamwork

Shocking as it may seem – or perhaps not in the least surprising! – many teams and divisions in companies don't really know what each other actually does. This could be as specific as a misunderstanding about individual job roles, to not understanding the role of an entire department. How then can a manager expect teams and divisions to draw effectively on each other's resources and skills, and work, quite simply, as a team? The following Mind Map exercise is a powerful way to improve team dynamics.

Exercise

1 Divide the teams or divisions into groups of approximately four people and ask each team or division to pick a team to mind map.

2 Each group then creates a Mind Map, starting with a central image that captures the team they are mind mapping.

3 Once the central image is in place, individual members of the group should complete their own quick-fire Mind Map, to allow them to explore what they currently know about the team.

4 The group should then come back together and create the basic ordering ideas from the central image. These could be organised along the lines of the various roles in the team or the objectives and outcomes of the team.

5 Once these are in place, the group should take a break, followed by another quick-fire Mind Map to integrate what they have learnt about the team from other members of the group, and from the main branches in place.

6 Now sub-branches are added, as well as any necessary codes.

7 Once the group is happy with the Mind Map, the whole team comes together to discuss what they do and don't know about the people they work with.

8 As this discussion can be very revealing, each group Mind Map should be revised and edited as the discussions go on. It may be that a second Mind Map emerges from these discussions, but it is important always to keep a record of the first – almost as a 'before' and 'after'.

Masanori Kanda, named Japan's top marketer in the November issue of *GQ Japan* (2006), is known as one of the most influential entrepreneurs in Japan today. He used a variation of the exercise above to create team synergy and improve performance in his company, Almacreations.

Eight teams representing eight divisions of Almacreations drew Mind Maps of the company's divisions on a large blank sheet of paper. Each team consisted of four to six people. After drawing the Mind Maps, participants were given the opportunity to look at the Mind Maps of other teams. In doing this, they found all sorts of ways to create fusion across the company – for example, that the marketing division should exchange information and ideas with the system development division to come up with creative ideas and solutions. This exercise also exposed the rationale of how each division was organised – and helped find solutions as to how this could, if necessary, be corrected.

Getting the point across with Mind Maps

Because Mind Maps are so visual and can have such a big impact, they are ideal for managers who need to get an important, even crucial, point across, quickly, clearly and, most importantly, memorably. The following examples show how this has been achieved and should inspire you to find ways of using Mind Maps to make direct, impactful communications to your team.

Snake-bite treatment

New Zealand has no live snakes; not even one in a zoo's secure display case. Live snakes are prohibited entry into New Zealand, as an introduced snake could breed and threaten the abundant bird life. Snakes can carry parasites or zoonotic diseases, capable of harming people or other reptiles, such as the endangered tuatara, our nearest link to the dinosaurs. Some snakes are venomous, presenting risks to other small animals and to people.

The Mind Map at the top of page 164 was devised by the New Zealand Ministry of Agriculture and Forestry's Biosecurity New Zealand (MAFBNZ) and the Department of Conservation to instruct people with no knowledge of snake-bite treatment, or first aid, who may have misconceptions about what to do. The wrong actions could be fatal. Bandaging technique is critical (and not removing it under any circumstances); correct bandaging should be learnt and practised. Its value to all quarantine officers working at the border, inspecting goods and people entering the country, became known.

Prickly heat

Top managers from the British Dispensary participated in a mind mapping workshop. They decided to mind map one of their best-known products, Snake Brand Prickly Heat Powder. The Mind Map they produced (shown at the bottom of page 164) outlined all the uses for the product and was so successful at getting ideas across, it was passed on to an advertising agency and became the creative force behind an ad campaign that year, '108 Ways to Manage Prickly Heat'.

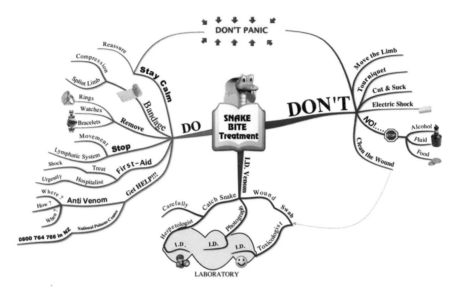

A draft Mind Map that breaks several Mind Map rules (can you spot them?) but nevertheless conveys effectively to field workers what to do and what not to do when dealing with snake bites

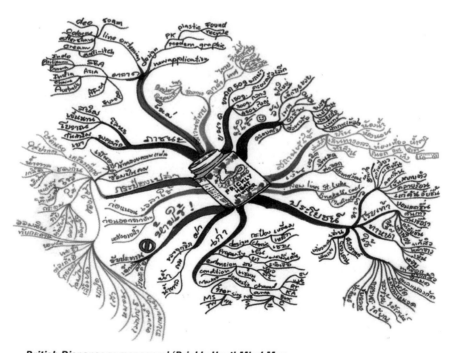

British Dispensary managers' 'Prickly Heat' Mind Map

Mind Maps in life, study and work

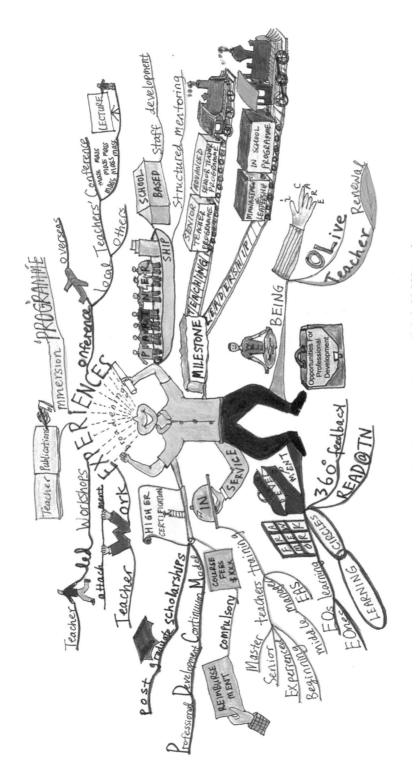

A Mind Map from the Singapore Ministry of education with which they communicate to all their 28,000 teachers

Mind Maps for management

Whether you're managing just a few people or big divisions and organisations, Mind Maps provide many ways to enhance teamwork, communication and strategy. Hopefully this chapter will have inspired you to apply them to your work, and if you want to look more deeply into this, *Mind Maps for Business* provides a detailed look at how Mind Maps can be used in business.

Now we turn to our final part, where we look at the radiant future of Mind Maps.

The concept and application of iMind Maps **really gels** with the way I **think about and execute** projects, meetings, tasks, processes and larger programmes. I know for a fact that it has increased my **productivity and innovation ability** and I am trying hard to spread the word around the organisation to '**take a chance on Buzan**'. The beautiful composition and structure of pictures, colourful, organic branches while also **linking to a project plan** really works for me.

Henning Dräger, Executive Assistant to Director, Friends of the Earth

Part 5
Mind Maps and the future

In this final part we take a close look at how Mind Maps have integrated with technology to form electronic Mind Maps. As well as exploring both the advantages and the disadvantages of mind mapping on a computer, you'll get a thorough grounding in how to actually *create* Mind Maps on a computer. This part, and the book, will conclude with a look to the future of the Mind Map and the brain.

Computer Mind Maps

This chapter introduces you to the computer Mind Map, exploring its most appropriate usage and the advantages and disadvantages of employing it for your mind mapping tasks. Lots of examples and references are included from the official Buzan mind mapping software, designed intuitively to reflect the principles of the traditional pen-and-paper Mind Map.

Whilst you work your way through this chapter, you may find it useful to download a free trial of iMindMap software from www.imindmap.com.

Why mind map on a computer?

> I'm the sort of person for whom linear planning is a real challenge, and I've produced hand drawn Mind Maps for years. The electronic version allows me to develop my ideas over time. It's been useful in my role here because I'm currently building a new programme of work, from scratch.
>
> RACHEL GOODE, Group Communications Director, Oxford University Press

Creating Mind Maps on a computer unleashes the exciting and vital capabilities for managing information in today's fast-paced post 'information age'. With the increasing amounts of information we have to deal with, and the speed at which we have to get through things, it is becoming much more critical to utilise the new brain-friendly technology and tools available.

Computer mind mapping has a pivotal role to play in bringing clarity to the vast amounts of information available to us. It helps us to gather, assimilate and integrate ideas and knowledge in a way that realises our full potential, whether in our personal lives or at work.

How can you mind map on a computer?

Computers are, at last, now getting ever closer to being able to reproduce the organic and interconnected nature of real human thought. iMindMap software can duplicate the visual variety, fluidity and portability that is offered by traditional pen-and-paper Mind Maps. For instance, you can create free-flowing branches by simply clicking and dragging your mouse or by drawing directly on to a tablet PC screen or Interactive Whiteboard. You can even sketch your own personal drawings to insert into your Mind Maps!

Computer software really comes into its own by offering a robust feature set which helps to boost your mental processes and productivity in any number of ways. There are many stand-alone software programs available as well as web-based applications, several of which will allow you to:

- Automatically generate neat and colourful Mind Maps.
- Edit and enhance your Mind Maps as much as you like.
- Analyse and manage your data at intricate levels using a range of tools.
- Share and present your Mind Maps through, for example, Outlook.
- Convert your Mind Maps into different communication and reporting formats.
- Organise, implement and track projects from start to finish.
- Link to external information sources.

Computer Mind Maps vs. traditional Mind Maps

Mind Maps can be applied to any situation that requires idea generation, information capture, problem-solving, decision-making, learning or organisation. The physical act of drawing a Mind Map often gives a hand-drawn Mind Map the creative edge over computer-based versions. However, computer-generated Mind Maps take things to a new productivity level by being faster to produce and permitting a higher degree of flexibility for many of the occasions when you wish to mind map. Clearly both hand-drawn and computer forms are important for personal, educational and professional productivity. On the next two pages are some examples of Computer Mind Maps.

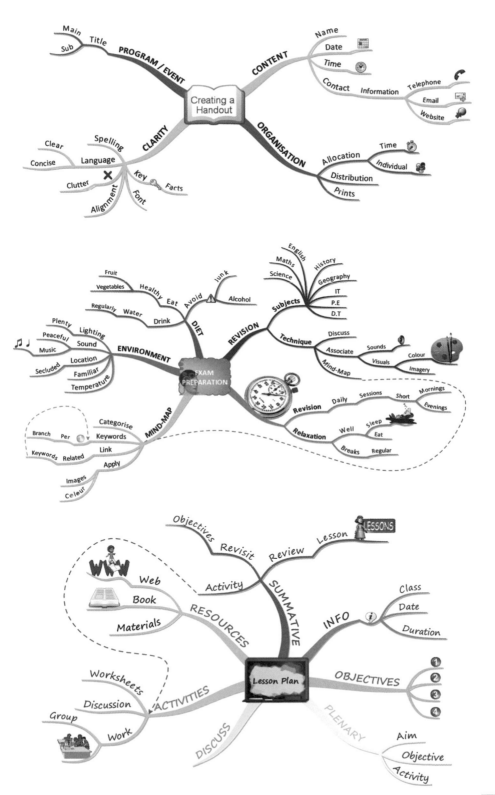

Creating a Handout

PROGRAM / EVENT
- Title — Main / Sub

CONTENT
- Name
- Date
- Time
- Contact — Information — Telephone / Email / Website

CLARITY
- Language — Spelling — Clear / Concise
- Clutter ✗ — Key — Facts
- Alignment — Font

ORGANISATION
- Allocation — Time / Individual
- Distribution
- Prints

EXAM PREPARATION

DIET
- Eat — Healthy — Fruit / Vegetables
- Drink — Water — Regularly
- Avoid — Junk / Alcohol

ENVIRONMENT
- Lighting — Plenty
- Sound — Peaceful / Music
- Location — Secluded / Familiar / Temperature

REVISION
- Subjects — English / Maths / History / Science / Geography / IT / P.E / D.T
- Technique — Discuss / Associate — Sounds / Visuals — Colour / Imagery / Mind-Map
- Revision — Daily — Sessions — Short — Mornings / Evenings
- Relaxation — Sleep — Well / Eat / Breaks — Regular

MIND-MAP
- Categorise
- Keywords — Branch — Per
- Link — Keywords — Related
- Apply — Images / Colour

Lesson Plan

SUMMATIVE
- Review — Lesson — LESSONS
- Revisit — Objectives
- Activity

RESOURCES
- Web — WWW
- Book
- Materials

ACTIVITIES
- Worksheets
- Discussion
- Group — Work

INFO (i)
- Class
- Date
- Duration

OBJECTIVES
- ① ② ③ ④

PLENARY
- Aim
- Objective
- Activity

DISCUSS

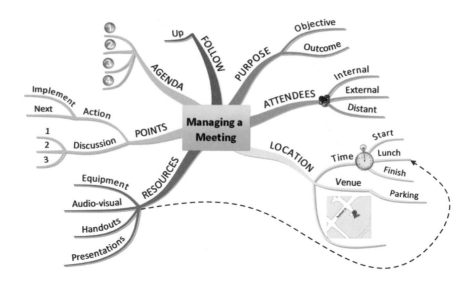

Benefits of computer Mind Maps

Computer Mind Maps offer several functional advantages over hand-drawn Mind Maps, extending the technique of mind mapping beyond its traditional capabilities. These advantages are set to lead computer Mind Maps into ever greater popularity.

1 Automatic Mind Map generation and enhancement

Creating a computer Mind Map is extremely simple and intuitive when using modern software applications. There are absolutely no space limitations – you will not reach the edge of your workspace as you would when mind mapping on paper! Buzan's iMindMap is the perfect software tool to demonstrate the ease with which you can generate your Mind Maps.

Central theme

The computer prompts you to create a central theme (image and title) and positions your chosen central theme in the centre of your screen.

Creating branches

You can opt to create your own organic free-flowing branches by clicking and dragging your mouse from the centre and inputting your topics. Alternatively, you can use 'Speed Mind Mapping' mode to create Mind Maps quickly using just your keyboard. For example, you type a title for your branch and hit 'Return' to reveal ready-shaped branches. You just think,

iMindMap on iPhone: Mobile technology now allows users to create Mind Maps anywhere at any time meaning that ideas are never missed or forgotten.

type and 'Return' and your Mind Map grows before your eyes! You don't have to worry about the precise order and placement of your ideas as your Mind Maps will automatically be structured for you, and you can then navigate between branches using just the arrow keys on your keyboard.

Layout, colours and fonts

Not only can you just let your ideas flow, you can personalise your Mind Map automatically with auto features. Shape your Mind Map instantly by choosing from a series of layout styles ranging from Linear to Organic to Radial, and use pre-customised settings to automatically apply branch colours and fonts for your branch text.

Images, highlights and relationships

When you have completed your free-flow ideas, you can go back to your Mind Map and enrich it with images, highlights and relationship arrows using the selection of features available to you. With regard to images, you are not just limited to pictures that you can draw; you can take advantage of an array of clipart, 3-D animations, photos, audio and video files that are readily available through the software or can be found on the web. Using the highlight cloud system you can instantly highlight different features of a complex Mind Map for emphasis. For example, you might surround all the 'expensive' options in a bright red cloud or all the 'great' ideas in a green cloud. All of these 'extras' will make your Mind Map more memorable, interesting and creative.

A further exciting option for automatically generating your Mind Maps involves 'digital ink'. You can hand draw your computer Mind Maps directly on to the screen of a Tablet PC or Interactive Whiteboard using a digital pen, as if you were using conventional pen and paper!

2 Effortless restructuring and editing

Once you have created your Mind Map, you can easily 'flex' and restructure it to make it more meaningful or to accommodate new insights and ideas. Mind mapping software lets you manipulate ideas and information with a level of freedom and flexibility that is unheard of in other types of application.

Adding, removing and moving branches

You can add, remove or move branches of key words around in seconds all via simple mouse-click operations. You can arrange and rearrange your topics until your Mind Map perfectly represents your ideas. This is virtually impossible to do in a hand-drawn Mind Map. Every time you change the position of a topic, you change its context and thereby stimulate your brain to think of new ideas and view different connections between the other ideas in your Mind Map.

Changing branch properties

Each branch property (shape, font or colour) can be individually changed or you can apply pre-customised styles. These elements can be reworked whenever you want to add new meaning or to recode your Mind Map.

Importing and editing

Many software programs allow you to import, save and edit pre-existing Mind Maps from other mind mapping applications. This saves you valuable time reproducing Mind Maps and enables you to use your preferred software program for customisation.

The key advantage here is that computer Mind Maps can be developed over an extended period of time and you won't ever need to redraw your Mind Map from scratch, even if you want to use it for a new purpose. You can create variations of the same Mind Map almost instantaneously.

3 Improved analysis and management of information

Computer Mind Maps allow you to interact with much more information than could be reasonably managed in a physical drawing. Indeed, your computer Mind Map is easily transformed into a serious knowledge management tool which is perfect for handling information overload and conducting in-depth analysis.

Navigation

An essential feature of computer Mind Maps is the ability to explore and navigate more widely without getting lost. Navigation functions provide a miniature outline of your Mind Map workspace, which you can use to move around large or multiple Mind Maps, zeroing in on any parts that you want to change.

Expand and collapse branches

The ability to expand and collapse branches allows you both to see an overview and to 'drill down' to a detailed view, in the same document. When you're working on a complex project, this capability is incredibly useful as you can store lots of information neatly in your Mind Map without being overwhelmed by it.

Focus in and out

You can temporarily 'focus in' on one branch, turning the selected branch into the central theme of a new Mind Map. Without the distractions of your original Mind Map, you can look at ideas and information at a more objective level and really concentrate on the new topic. All in all, this is an invaluable stimulus for innovative thinking.

Searching

Many Mind Map programs allow you to search the contents of your Mind Map or multiple Mind Maps for key words or phrases. By changing the focus of your Mind Map to the searched content, this function can help you question and analyse your Mind Map more effectively and give you more meaningful insight into its content. It is an extremely useful facility if you are working on a large, complex Mind Map with lots of information.

4 The ability to create a 'visual database' – adding information

Using single key words to briefly present topics per branch is essential to a good Mind Map, as it opens up new avenues of thought. However, sometimes you may need to write sentences of explanation for yourself or others, or to refer to more detailed information sources on your computer, an intranet or the Internet. Computer Mind Maps allow you to do this and to keep the extra information hidden until it is needed, transforming your Mind Map into a structured, visual front-end for your information sources. By avoiding clutter and providing fast, easy access to your resources, your computer Mind Map becomes an essential way to handle information overload.

Notes

You can add notes to any branch of your Mind Map using a 'Notes Editor' window with full word processing capability. The content of the note can be as much or as little as you need to ensure that you or the reader under-stands the key messages.

Links

You can attach attributes such as documents, websites, URLs, applications, other Mind Maps and folders on your computer to any branch. There is no limit to the number of links you can add to a branch, helping you collate information from a variety of sources for improved understanding. You just click for fast access to all your supporting information.

These capabilities are ideal for work and study. When you are studying, you can keep all your learning content connected to your Mind Map and once you have 'learned' it, you will only need the key words on your Mind Map to recall it. At work, you will have a knowledge database that means you'll spend less time looking for key documents and information and more time on achieving your goals.

5 Superior organisation and task implementation

You can use computer Mind Maps as a highly efficient front-end process for all tasks that require organisation, such as new projects, to create meeting agendas and to-do lists. However, software produced Mind Maps aren't only useful at the beginning of a task; they can become a powerful tool for managing projects and tracking progress on an ongoing basis. Many soft-ware packages contain fully integrated project management systems to organise any type of project from planning a party, managing a budget to product development processes.

Project management tools

You can identify key project tasks in your Mind Map and attach detailed infor-mation to each task – including start and end dates, duration, milestones,

Mind Maps and the future

priorities and completion percentage. Conventional project management tools such as Gantt charts and timelines are often fully integrated in the software so that you can view project progress, and your project data can also be exported to Microsoft Project for further manipulation.

Simple task management

Some software tools support effective resource allocation for project tasks. For instance, you can import relevant contacts from Microsoft Outlook and assign them to project tasks. Once allocated, you can export tasks and milestone information to Outlook, with all details emailed to the appropriate contacts. You are then free to follow up actions until they are complete via Microsoft Outlook.

6 Supports effective collaboration and teamworking

Computer Mind Maps support various modes of group collaboration, helping you to channel collective creativity and brain power in an effective manner.

For example, if you are working on Mind Map content that has to go through an approval cycle or you have the beginnings of an idea and want others to flesh it out, you can use computer Mind Maps to obtain input from team members or colleagues. Distribute your Mind Map electronically to the target recipients for their review or upload the Mind Map to a shared workspace. Each contributor can mark their comments with special identifying attributes so that when the Mind Maps are returned to you, each person's input can be extracted and merged into one Mind Map. For ongoing projects, it is a good idea to establish a visual vocabulary which defines the standard use of symbols, colours and styles for Mind Maps that are shared. By developing a shared understanding of what they mean with your team members, you can then use these visual enhancements consistently.

A group can assemble around a computer Mind Map that is projected on to a large screen and work on it together. This is a productive method for team meetings or group brainstorming sessions. Seeing ideas and information recorded 'live' within the context of the session gives the computer Mind Map a degree of potency that cannot be matched using flip charts and coloured pens.

Whichever collaboration method is used, computer Mind Maps can offer all team members the ability to see the 'big picture' and provide their input in a friendly and engaging manner. They also work to speed up considerably the time it takes to gain agreement or consensus.

7 Numerous sharing and distribution options

A computer-generated Mind Map has an attractive, high-quality appearance which can be used to share vital knowledge with others. Software programs offer a variety of options for making your Mind Maps quickly available to other people:

- *Printing* – If you want to provide hard copy Mind Maps then print options allow you to print your Mind Maps in a variety of formats. For example, single/multiple pages, with colour or black and white, with headers or without, as a text outline, etc.

- *Image* – You can export a copy of your Mind Map as an image file (JPEG, Bitmap, etc.) and even choose the quality of your image.

- *Web page* – You can export your Mind Map as a web page which can then be placed on a website for others to view.

- *Scaleable Vector Graphics (SVG)* – This option is ideal if you want to export your Mind Map to excellent high quality graphics. You can use these graphics in posters, books, packages such as Adobe Illustrator or post them on the web.

- *Adobe PDF* – You can export your Mind Map as an Adobe PDF file which creates a read-only version of your Mind Map along with links and notes that others can easily view. The PDF file format is the universal standard for electronic document distribution worldwide.

9 Various modes of presentation

A powerful advantage of mind mapping software is that you can employ it as an active tool to present your ideas, something that is more difficult to do with a hand-drawn Mind Map. There are various ways that you can deliver impressive and lively presentations using software: expanding branches one by one; giving interactive presentations; and/or focusing on specific topics.

Expanding branches one by one

By collapsing all branches of your Mind Map initially, you can present by expanding branches one level at a time. Exposing the contents of your Mind Map incrementally keeps your audience focused on the topic at hand. You can control how much information is revealed at any one time, reducing the possibility of overwhelming your audience.

Interactive Mind Map presentations

In Buzan's iMindMap software, you are able to present your material as an animated Mind Map. Each branch is treated as one presentation slide which has been pre-set to flow in a specific sequence. This method really brings your Mind Map to life and captivates your audience!

'Focusing' on specific topics

Using 'Focus in and Focus out' tools, you can temporarily zoom in on one particular branch of your Mind Map, turning it into a new central idea. This is great for encouraging audience participation as you can add their thoughts and ideas to new branches linked to your focused topic.

The advantages of using mind mapping software for your presentations do not stop at the end of your presentation. Indeed, you can ensure that your material is readily available on the Internet for the audience to access after your presentation. You can easily export your Mind Map to websites and attach additional information to the branches, such as files or web links, to help your audience follow up on the information they are interested in. All of this takes mind mapping software on to a whole new spectrum of interactivity.

Employing mind mapping software as an active tool in presentations

10 Converts to conventional forms of communication and reporting

In the modern business world, it is not really acceptable to present your colleagues or manager with a coloured paper drawing of your plans or updates. Business decisions are based on reports, proposals, presentations and project plans. A computer-generated Mind Map eliminates this problem as it can be transformed into a variety of professional formats at the click of a button. For example, you can export your Mind Maps as Word documents, PowerPoint presentations, spreadsheets and Microsoft Project plans. So, for the times when your colleagues, managers or clients expect a document, spreadsheet, presentation or project plan, you don't need to put in mountains of additional work – the software does the work for you.

For instance, using Buzan's iMindMap software you are able to convert your Mind Maps using the following export options:

- *Text document* – You can export your Mind Map as a formatted text outline in Microsoft Word or OpenOffice Writer.

- *Spreadsheet* – If you have a Mind Map containing financial projections, costings, sales reports or other financial data, you can export it as a spreadsheet in Microsoft Excel or OpenOffice Calc.

- *Presentation* – You can export your Mind Map as a standard 'slide-show' presentation or animated one-slide Mind Map presentation to applications like Microsoft PowerPoint, OpenOffice Impress or Mac Keynote.

- *Project plans* – Export your project Mind Maps to Microsoft Project where you can perform advanced project analysis using the application's features.

The ability to export is an immensely powerful benefit and positions mind mapping where it is most beneficial, as the creative front-end of the extensive variety of tasks that business and professional people are required to perform. Your computer Mind Map becomes the starting place to form and structure your ideas for almost any type of project or task.

When should you use computer mind mapping?

Computer Mind Maps are much more than a simple visual representation of ideas. They provide excellent facilities for rapidly generating, reorganising and structuring ideas and information, and for collaborating with others. As such, there are several business, educational and personal activities for which computer Mind Maps are particularly invaluable. The following are just some examples.

Meetings

Mind mapping software can be used to manage all aspects of meetings from setting the agenda to capturing notes during the meeting and distributing notes or minutes to the participants afterwards.

You can mind map the agenda and circulate it to attendees in advance of the meeting in a standard, easily accessible format such as PDF. Most mind mapping software tools allow you to print, email or export your Mind Map to other applications for simple and rapid distribution to others. During the meeting, you can use the agenda Mind Map as a template quickly to capture information and notes without having to worry about the legibility of your writing or its presentation. Whether you are taking notes for yourself, or minutes for the whole meeting, a computer Mind Map can clearly encapsulate the shape and structure of the meeting, the relative importance of individual points and the way facts and ideas that arise relate to each other. As you are not tied to the spatial limitations of a piece of paper or flip chart, you have the freedom to add ideas and expand your Mind Map as much as you need.

After the meeting, minutes of a meeting taken in Mind Map form can be distributed to attendees in record time, helping you take advantage of the impetus created in the meeting.

Brainstorming

Computer mind mapping is ideal for brainstorming. Using 'Speed Mind Mapping' mode you can immediately transfer all your ideas straight on to a Mind Map. Your branches are automatically created for you so you don't have to worry about structure and hierarchy; you just let your ideas flow. You can always revise and rearrange your Mind Map later and you never have to recreate your Mind Map from scratch.

Mind mapping software also opens up new creative opportunities for group brainstorming sessions that don't exist with hand-drawn Mind Maps. Ideas can be recorded and displayed on a computer Mind Map, which is projected on to a screen, allowing groups to form a 'creative huddle' around the Mind Map so that creative juices flow easily.

I started using iMindMap software after our development director introduced me to it. I use it to brainstorm and group together new ideas, thoughts and actions etc. to develop our strategic plans, projects and policies, especially after planning days.

Our sport is multi disciplined and there are so many facets to what we do – planning and collecting all our ideas, skills and thoughts are essential.

DAVID MCNALLY, Chief Executive Officer, Welsh Gymnastics

BRAINSTORMING

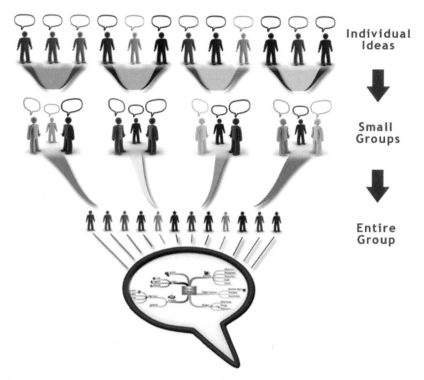

Individual Ideas

Small Groups

Entire Group

Computer mind mapping is ideal for brainstorming

Negotiation

Whether you are buying a house, selling a new product or securing a business venture, computer Mind Maps can help you chart your way through each stage of a negotiation successfully, increasing the chance that the outcome will be positive for both parties.

Not only can you use computer Mind Maps as a framework for ensuring you prepare well for the negotiation; you can also use a computer Mind Map during the negotiation session to help you manage the whole process with confidence. Your mind mapping software can be utilised as a presentation device to simply state your case to the other party in a clear and compelling manner. Or, with participation from the other party, you can create a Mind Map template to structure and record the entire negotiation, using it as a tool to reach a conclusion that satisfies both parties. The template Mind Map can be prepared in advance or at the beginning of the negotiation and filled in during the course of the session, with both parties making their contributions.

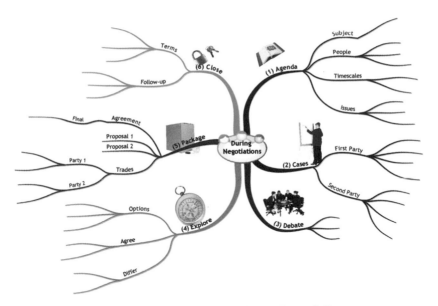

A Mind Map can be usefully used to structure and record negotiations

Using mind mapping software really speeds up the finalisation of the negotiation as well. There no longer needs to be a delay while confirmation of the deal is written up. Mind Maps can be quickly printed so both parties walk away with a fully signed-off record of the negotiation.

Personal goal setting

Mind mapping software is perfect for engaging yourself in the process of setting your life's future direction. You can use it not only to define your goals and implementation plans, but also to monitor and track your progress.

For each main role or function in your life (for example, work, family, etc.), you can mind map your long-term goals and break them down into different short-term goals. With an array of numbering, symbol, connecting and highlighting options available to you in the software, you can easily assign priorities to each goal, and link goals to other roles or functions. You don't have to stop at just goals. Mind mapping software gives you the capacity to include the 'who, what, when, where and why' elements that are required to achieve the goal, and to attach notes to branches with extra detail. If necessary, you can link to Mind Maps where you can become involved in more detailed planning.

Many mind mapping programs now offer excellent project management facilities, which allow you to outline timescales, milestones and the priorities associated with a key goal. Your percentage of completion on each goal can be easily tracked, turning your Mind Map into an ongoing, interactive personal record of achievement.

Strategy development

A computer Mind Map can be an excellent tool for formulating and laying out the strategy of a company. Starting with a central vision of the company, a computer Mind Map can be used to outline attractively the strategies and objectives by which that vision will be realised. After scoping out the long- and short-term strategies of the company, you can use the extensive features of your software to drill down into the Mind Map, filling in the particulars of each strategy using attachments, notes and links to more detailed Mind Maps.

Strategy Mind Maps also provide great unifying overviews for members of staff. Using software, you can easily export your strategy Mind Map into a standard business file format such as PDF and distribute it company-wide to give direction and inspiration to employees.

Project management

Many software packages provide you with everything you need to manage all types of project, from the initial planning stages through to reporting on final results.

By mind mapping out your projects using software, you can store all your project information in one place to help you stay focused and organised. Information such as ideas, project objectives, questions, research needs, team roles and responsibilities can all be included, with links to other project-related resources (such as websites, documents, reports) that you or colleagues may need to access quickly. By attaching notes to branches, you can store additional information out of view until you are ready to look at it.

Using the project management functions that are available in many software packages you can also define project milestones and track the progress of key elements of the project. By checking the 'percentage complete' stage of each task, you can determine your progress at a glance.

If you want to use Mind Maps frequently for project planning and management, you can streamline your workload by using mind mapping software to create a project template Mind Map that can act as a starting point for each new project. Not only will this save you valuable time, but it will also ensure that you always gather all of the required information for each new project.

iMindMap is one of the most useful organisation tools that I use on a daily basis. I use it whenever I want to gather my thoughts, ranging from training sessions to managing projects. When I use it in meetings or in presentations, people have commented on how the topics were easier to understand with the Mind Maps. iMindMap is really an invaluable tool in helping me succeed at work.

NEIL QUIOGUE, Information Security, PopCap Games International

Performance appraisals

Using mind mapping software offers several benefits when conducting performance appraisals. It removes paper-based constraints, brings greater consistency to the appraisal process and reduces time delays.

You can provide a simple structure for appraisals by preparing a colour-coded Mind Map template, which can be used to evaluate an employee's strengths, weak performance areas and training or development needs. This template Mind Map can then be open on a laptop and filled in during the course of the appraisal, with both the manager and the employee making their contributions. Unlike its paper counterpart, a computer Mind Map appraisal can go into as much depth as needed simply by adding more sub-branches or by attaching notes with detailed information to specific branches. The use of a template also brings consistency to the whole appraisal process by streamlining its implementation across all employees.

The use of software makes it easier to adapt your appraisal structures to different requirements, bringing greater value to your management duties and your human resources department. For example, you can create Mind Map templates that focus on more specific skills and capabilities, such as Technical, Management, Job skills, Productivity, Personal qualities and Communication.

Finally, using mind mapping software speeds up the whole appraisal process. The appraisee doesn't have to wait for the write up – they can walk away with a printout of their performance evaluation Mind Map or can be emailed a copy immediately after the appraisal, enabling them to set in motion immediately the necessary training and development.

Group collaboration/teamworking

A computer-generated Mind Map is the perfect tool for collaborating with others to develop a variety of plans or implement projects such as new product development processes. It is particularly valuable for gaining the 'buy-in' from everyone involved to ensure a plan or project receives maximum support.

You can harness the input of key people by emailing them a Mind Map that you've created for their review or by uploading it to a shared workspace where other team members can contribute their ideas or comments.

Furthermore, you can use integrated project management functions to add weight to the collaboration process by including milestones, priorities and 'percentage complete' detail on each main task.

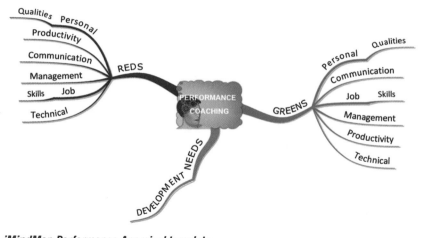

iMindMap Performance Appraisal template

By involving others in the active development of the computer Mind Map, they are more likely to understand the benefits of undertaking key strategies and to be enthusiastic about implementing certain tasks.

Life management

Mind mapping software can be effectively utilised as an 'information dashboard' to help people organise their personal and professional lives.

You can generate a 'dashboard' Mind Map that acts as a central base for all aspects of your life, providing a summary of key information such as your calendar, contacts, ideas, key documents or files, major projects, important things to remember and so on. Each of these main topics can contain notes or links to other relevant information sources. You can even link branches to sub Mind Maps that are focused on each major area.

Your software effectively consolidates all the data that you need to manage into a single visual Mind Map, and the beauty of it is that it can be organised in countless ways to suit your personal preferences and specific purposes.

Computer Mind Maps in the future

Up to now computer mind mapping software has brought us excellent capabilities for increasing our personal and professional productivity. It provides a creative way to bring information together and encourages us to manage our attention more effectively. So, as technology continues its progress, what can we expect from computer mind mapping in the future? Here we explore some exciting developments that will bring more sophistication and flexibility to mind mapping.

'Hands free' mind mapping

The latest developments in software support integration with voice-recognition technology will bring a new voice-activated dimension to mind mapping. You will be able to use a library of voice commands to add, edit topics and sub-topics, icons and so on, freeing you from having to type using a PC keyboard or navigate with a mouse. Speech technology and mind mapping software will form a powerful productivity combination which will invigorate the way meetings and brainstorming sessions are conducted and will help people save time and conquer information overload. It also creates a level playing field for people with disabilities, liberating them to organise their thoughts and communicate their ideas to others.

Going mobile

With rapid technological progress bringing more powerful hand-held computers and mobile phones, the way is becoming clear for us to equip them with computer mind mapping software. Computer mind mapping will go truly mobile! You will be able to generate and edit Mind Maps using your mobile phone or hand-held computer and transmit them immediately to the intended recipients. This development will bring greater incorporation of mind mapping into our daily lives.

Convergence of web/desktop mind mapping

Many software packages are based around a desktop mind mapping experience. With the increasing prominence and accessibility of the Internet, the future will see more of a convergence between web-based and desktop applications. For instance, as well as being able to conduct web searches and online database queries from within desktop software, you will also be able to access and edit your Mind Maps anywhere through a combination of desktop and web-based applications. Seamless integration will allow you to work on a Mind Map off-line and for it to be automatically synchronised with your online file once you connect to the Internet.

Stronger database connections

Mind mapping software will be able to connect, via security, to corporate databases such Customer Relationship Management (CRM) and Material Requirements Planning (MRP) systems, enabling you to seamlessly search for and extract relevant data into your Mind Maps. This is an especially valuable feature for complex project Mind Maps that consolidate a wealth of information and will surely elevate Mind Map 'dashboards' to the next level.

Improved mechanisms for collaboration

The productivity potential of computer mind mapping will be enhanced by the ability of users of Mind Map software to share the full contents of their Mind Maps with others, without the need for each person to have a full licensed copy of the software or a file viewer. Others will even be able to edit your Mind Map, opening up greater collaboration opportunities.

Web 2.0 connections

Mind mapping software will be able to interact with next generation Web 2.0 tools, such as social networking (Facebook, etc.), blogging and user generated video (YouTube). These tools encourage mass participation and collaboration and are changing the way people communicate. Mind Map software will reflect this by allowing you to engage with others to pull selected content from these tools into your Mind Maps.

Computer mind mapping clearly has an exciting future ahead of it. The ever-increasing power of computing will bring even greater levels of flexibility and freedom to mind mapping software users. Mind Map technology will mature enough to become the instrument of choice for individuals and companies seeking to undertake just about any task, unleashing their potential to achieve their key objectives and visions.

With the growth in tandem of machine and human intelligence, what is our most likely and possible future? Some possibilities have already been highlighted above. In the final chapter I give my personal perspective on mental literacy, Mind Maps and the future.

The future is radiant

A mentally literate world is one in which every individual is aware of the inherent brilliance that lies waiting to be unleashed in every human brain. It is a world in which everyone knows the exquisite and phenomenal structures and functions of the brain, and is aware of the processes and applications of the extraordinary cognitive skills, including especially memory, creativity, learning and all forms of thinking. I discovered the Mind Map as a way to help people to realise, access and use the astounding power of their brain.

The most beautiful intricate mysterious complex and powerful object in the known universe, your brain, is reflected in the natural architecture of a Nebula

The learning revolution

As this book goes to press, over five decades after the Mind Map was first conceived, I can proudly look back and marvel at the revolution in learning that has and is taking place, in which, I believe, the Mind Map has played an integral role.

Brain Stars

The twentieth century started with film stars, and rapidly moved on to singing stars, rock stars, pop stars and sports stars. The twenty-first, the Century of the Brain, has already begun with Brain Stars who demonstrate the principle of a healthy mind in a healthy body. Gary Kasparov, the athletic and dynamic World Chess Champion, has millions of children around the world pinning posters of him on the walls of their rooms and dreaming of becoming international chess Grandmasters and champions.

Similarly, the charming young Hungarian girl Judit Polgar, the youngest ever chess Grandmaster, is becoming a cult figure. Dominic O'Brien, the first, six-time and reigning World Memory Champion, who uses Memory Mind Maps to help him recall record-breaking amounts of data, now regularly appears on international television. And there is Raymond Keene, game master and world record holder for books written on games and thinking (100+!). Through his Mind Maps, articles, books and television presentations he has built up a following of 180,000 people who stay up until 1am to watch his programmes. Other members of this growing 'Charge of the Bright Brigade' include Edward De Bono, who travels around the world speaking to vast audiences about lateral thinking, and Stephen Hawking, the Cambridge physicist, whose book *A Brief History of Time* has, to date, been on the bestseller lists for longer than any other book in the history of publishing. Also included but sadly passed away were Carl Sagan, famous astronomer and leader of the billion-dollar-plus search for extraterrestrial intelligence, Omar Sharif, whose brilliance as a bridge player even outshone his career as an actor, and the extraordinary polymath and Professor of mathematics, 65-year-old Dr Marion Tinsley. Tinsley, disproving all the myths about age and mental abilities, was the world Number One World Draughts/Checkers Champion from 1954, during which time he lost only seven games. In 1992 he beat the world's new Number Two player, Chinook, a computer programme. Stating that he was using only a small part of his brain's Radiant Thinking abilities, Tinsley crushed a computer that could calculate three million moves a minute, and which had a database of over 27 billion positions! Paralleling this trend is the growing popularity of intellectual quiz programmes such as Brain of Britain and Mastermind, and the establishment of prizes such as the Brain Trust's 'Brain of the Year', most recently awarded to Baroness Susan Greenfield for her work on the human brain and for bringing her scientific endeavours to the public.

Teaching

Mind Maps are ideal for teachers planning lessons, not least in one of the fastest-growing areas of learning at the moment: language training. Mind Maps can be designed to stimulate the minds of the students to ask questions during the course of teaching, to encourage discussion and to indicate activity. This Mind Map shows how Mind Maps can be used specifically for the teaching of grammar. The Mind Map by Lars Soderberg, a Swedish master linguist and teacher, incorporates a comprehensive overview of the main elements of French grammar on a single page. In a single 'visual grasp' the Mind Map takes that which for many is considered difficult, if not impossible, and makes it clear and easily accessible.

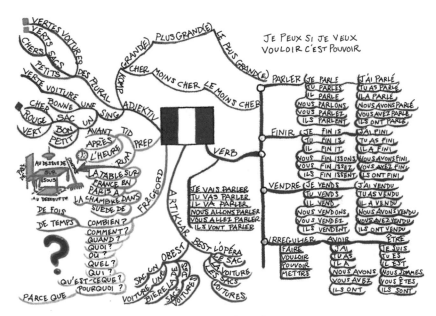

Lars Soderberg's Mind Map of an overview of French grammar

Special education

Mind Maps are particularly useful for helping those with learning disabilities. The Mind Map below was done by the author in conjunction with a nine-year-old boy we shall call 'Timmy'. Timmy suffered from fairly severe Cerebral Palsy, which meant that his motor functions were significantly impaired. He was considered by many to be ineducable and unintelligent.

When spending an afternoon with him surrounded by coloured crayons and blank notepaper, Tony first asked him to say who his family was. As notes were made Timmy watched intently, even correcting a fairly complicated spelling of his sister's name. Timmy was then asked what his main interests were, and without hesitation he said, 'space and dinosaurs', so these were put down as major branches of the Mind Map. Timmy was asked what he liked about space. He said, 'the planets'. Timmy then concisely named the planets in their correct order showing that he not only had a far better grasp of our local solar system than 90 per cent of the population, but that his picture of it was clear. When Timmy got to the planet Saturn, he paused, looked straight into Tony's eyes and said, 'L-U-H-V-L-E-Y . . .'

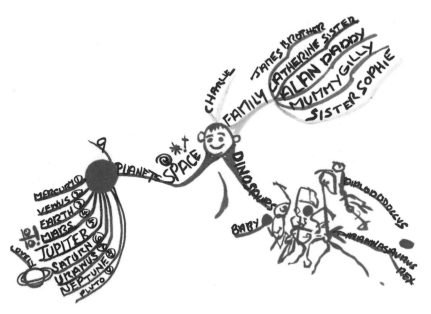

Mind Map by 'Timmy' with the help of Tony Buzan, demonstrating the abilities and knowledge of the 'learning disabled'

When it came to discussing the dinosaurs, Timmy asked for the pencil and did a quick scribbled drawing. Knowing that such scribbles are never meaningless, Tony asked him to explain what it meant. Timmy explained that it was, fairly obviously, a diplodocus and a tyrannosaurus rex: father, mother and baby. Timmy's mind was as bright and clear as any good university student's, his only difficulty being between the wiring of his thought and his physical expression of it.

He asked to do his own Mind Map. He produced another 'scribble' and explained it as follows: the orange represented his body, which made him very happy. The black squiggle in the top section represented his brain, which made him very happy. The yellow squiggle represented those parts of his own body which did not work, which made him unhappy. He paused for a moment and finally added a dark squiggle covering the bottom of the Mind Map, which he said represented how he was going to use his thinking to help make his body work better.

In this and many other such cases, the Mind Map frees the 'learning disabled' brain from semantic restrictions which often increase the disability if there is one, and may even create one where, in the beginning, there was not.

This revolution in learning and desire to learn has been realised in the ongoing success of The Festival of the Mind. Together with Ray Keene, I started this in 1995, with the intention of bringing people together to compete, brain to brain, on the key mental skills areas of memory, creativity, IQ and speed reading. The first festival attracted over 3,000 entrants from 50 countries, and since then four festivals have been held with over 30,000 entrants from at least 74 countries. As well as this, we also run separate world championships focusing on memory and chess – and, as with The Festival of the Mind, the popularity and high level of mental literacy showcased at these events is astounding.

This drive to improve our thinking, to release our mental powers, also comes at a time when we are being bombarded from every direction with swathes of information. Whether it's print or electronic, every day our brains somehow have to deal with insurmountable amounts of data. As we struggle to gather information into meaningful and manageable clusters, there still begs a question as to what we actually do with all this information – how do we actually process it in such a way that it is beneficial? The answer is, and will always be, found within each one of us, and now, more so than ever before, is the time to nurture and grow our most important asset, our brains.

A number of governments have already caught on to this and have decided to make fostering intelligence a primary national goal. To cite just a few examples: Singapore has committed itself to the development of mental literacy throughout its education system; it has also given itself the motto: 'Thinking Schools; Intelligent Nation'. Malaysia's Prime Minister and government have launched a 'brain revolution' initiative in which every child, by the year 2020, is to become conversant with all its 'brain skills'. In Mexico, the former President, Vincente Fox, proclaimed to 15,000 delegates at the Annual United Nations Conference on Creativity and Innovation that the twenty-first century would be officially known as the century for the 'development of intelligence, creativity and innovation'.

The Mentally Literate individual

In our historically 'mentally illiterate state', the mind of the individual is imprisoned in a relatively small conceptual framework, without the use of even the most primary Mental Literacy tools with which to help expand this conceptual framework. Even traditionally 'well-educated' and literate individuals are significantly restricted by the fact that they are able to use only a fraction of the biological and conceptual thinking tools which are available.

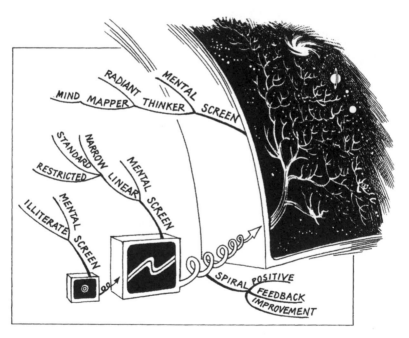

Illustration showing relative sizes of the 'mental screens' of the illiterate, linear and radian thinking minds. The radiant thinker's automatic self-enhancing feedback loop allows the screen the possibility of becoming infinitely large

Cognitive amplification

The Mentally Literate human is capable of turning on the radiant synergetic thinking engines, and creating conceptual frameworks and new paradigms of limitless possibility. The illustration on page 196 shows the 'mental screens' of the illiterate, the linear, and the Radiant Thinking mind. It can be seen that this last screen, by the nature of the intellectual machinery which drives it, continues to grow with an infinite possibility for size and dimension. It is the Radiant Thinker's automatic self-enhancing feedback loop which allows this massive intellectual freedom, and which reflects the inherent ability of each individual's brain – a formidable powerhouse, compact, efficient and beautiful, with potentially limitless horizons.

Applying Radiant Thinking principles to the brain enables you to range more freely among the major intellectual activities of making choices, remembering and creative thinking. Knowing the architecture of your thinking allows you to make choices and decisions using not only your conscious mental processes, but also your paraconscious – those vast continents, planets, galaxies and mental universes waiting to be explored by those who are Mentally Literate.

The Mentally Literate individual is also able to see the vital powerhouses of memory and creative thinking for what they really are: virtually identical mental processes that simply occupy different places in time. Memory is the re-creation in the present, of the past. Creativity is the projection, from the present, into the future, of a similar mental construct. The conscious development of memory or creativity through Mind Maps automatically increases the strength of both.

The most effective way for the individual to develop Mental Literacy skills, and to amplify the cognitive screen, is to follow the Radiant Thinking guidelines. The guidelines are a training ground for the development of mental skills such as those used by the 'Great Brains'. Indeed Leonardo da Vinci, arguably the greatest all-round user of mental abilities, devised a four-part formula for the development of a fully functioning, Mentally Literate brain that reflects these guidelines perfectly.

Leonardo da Vinci's Principles for the Development of a Mentally Literate Mind:

1 Study the science of art.

2 Study the art of science.

3 Develop your senses – especially learn how to see.

4 Realise that everything connects to everything else.

In modern Mind Mapping terms, da Vinci was saying to the individual:

Develop all your cortical skills, develop the entire range of your brain's receiving mechanisms, and realise that your brain operates synergetically and is an infinite and radiant association machine in a radiant universe.

By applying the Mind Map guiding principles and da Vinci's laws, the brain can develop its own individual expressions, exploring undreamed of domains. As Professor Petr Anokhin concluded:

There is no human being alive or who has ever lived who has even remotely explored the full potential of the brain. We therefore accept no restrictive limitations on the potential of the human brain – it is infinite!

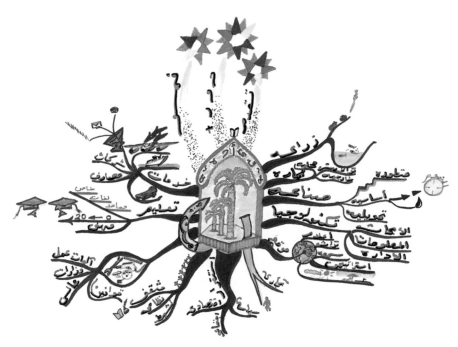

Mind Map by Sheikh Hamad outlining a plan for a Mentally Literate society

The Mentally Literate society

This Mind Map, by Sheikh Hamad the Arabian philosopher and thinker, out-lines a plan for the development of a Mentally Literate society. Demonstrating its pan-linguistic nature, the Mind Map covers the stabilising roots of educa-tion, economy and politics, and includes the other major factors of agriculture, services, operating mechanisms, industry, communication and marketing.

On the right-hand side of the Map, 'Information Technology' is emphasised because it is becoming more and more important in the way modern societies communicate and conduct business. On the left-hand side of the Map, the 'Education' branch shows two eyes with hats on them facing each other.

As Sheikh Hamad says:

This is a strong depiction for the need to educate the educators. This task has been neglected by many countries who fail to see the enormous importance of it. A good plan can only be successful if modifications can be applied at any stage. Therefore, the plan should be flexible and dynamic; it must be alive.

One of the interesting things about this particular Mind Map is that, during the early stages, a young waitress took a quick look at it, and when asked what she thought she saw, replied: 'It's a picture about making a better world.' She did not read the Arabic language, nor did she know beforehand what the subject was. This is a clear and vivid example of the success of the Mind Map as a basic communication tool, and of the importance of the application of research on how a human brain works.

The Mentally Literate family

In a Mentally Literate family, the emphasis will be on growth, communication, learning, creativity and love, in a context in which each family member realises and cherishes the miraculous, radiant and indescribably complex individuals who are the other members of that same family.

As John Rader Platt has said:

If this property of complexity could somehow be transformed into visible brightness so that it would stand forth more clearly to our senses, the biological world would become a walking field of light compared to the physical world. The sun with its great eruptions would fade to a pale simplicity compared to a rose bush, an earthworm would be a beacon, a dog would be a city of light, and human beings would stand out like blazing suns of complexity, flashing bursts of meaning to each other through the dull night of the physical world between. We would hurt each other's eyes. Look at the haloed heads of your rare and complex companions.
Is it not so?

It is so.

As the focus on and need to improve brain power increases, so does the role and importance of the Mind Map. We have seen that the Mind Map mimics the beautiful, awesome, moving, searching and persistent brain cell, of which we all have billions, and, as such, is our external mirror and key to unlocking our very own powerhouse of creativity, memory and thinking. *The Mind Map Book* is your guide to realising this – your greatest potential – and is my gift to you.

As I started with my dreams of a mentally literate world, I'd like to leave you with a real story about an extraordinary group of people who, like me, believe this dream is well on the way to becoming a reality.

The world's largest Mind Map

The sight of the world's largest Mind Map (see page 203) – a Mind Map a staggering three storeys high and four storeys wide – is one I hardly imagined until I had the incredible privilege of working with a team of thousands of individuals in Singapore to make the dream of a mentally literate world become increasingly true.

Henry Toi and his team, including Thum Cheng Cheong, Pang Ee Wei, Eric Cheong, Edward Nathan, Muhammad Mubarak, Tan Chew Ling and Tan Kwan Liang, in conjunction with the Singapore Institute of Management (SIM), all worked passionately to get the Mind Map from the drawing pad to the high-rise facade.

It was Henry who, in the manner of a true genius, overcame innumerable 'impossibilities' and made the impossible real. When he initially shared his idea to create the largest Mind Map in the world, people said he was 'crazy'. Technical difficulties, regulatory, logistical and human resource issues became a nightmare, but he passionately persisted.

The Mind Map celebrated not only the magnificence of the human mind and the accomplishments of the giant team (including 1,860 school children) who worked to make that dream come true. It is also a tribute to the extraordinary 42-year history of the tiny nation of Singapore, which has used its brain power to become one of the leading and most respected nations on our planet.

How the world's largest Mind Map was created

1 The first step was to develop an outline of the story that needed to be told on the Mind Map. This was initially conceptualised by Henry Toi.

2 The story was then redrawn as a Mind Map by Thum Cheng Cheong as a first draft.

3 The draft was circulated to the committee who scrutinised the Mind Map for both relevance and factual accuracy. Several changes were made.

4 The final draft was then handed to Vincent Chow of StudioWorkz Productions, who was tasked to vector the drawing on to computer.

5 The vectored file was then delivered to Dennis Kuang of Actaliz Marketing and Communications, who was tasked to print them into large canvas sheets.

6 The printed sheets were then inspected and allocated to each of the 15 participating schools (Bedok Primary School, CHIJ Our Lady of Good Council, Chong Boon Secondary School, Compassvale Secondary School, Coral Secondary School, First Toa Payoh Secondary School, Haig Girl's School, Jign Shan Primary School, Jurongville Scondary School, Kuo Chuan Presbyterian Primary School, Ngee Ann Primary School, Pei Hwa Presbyterian Primary School, Peixin Primary School, Rulang Primary School, Yuan Ching Secondary School).

7 The school students coloured up the Mind Map sheets and returned them to the committee, who then inspected each piece before handing them back to Dennis for sewing and fixing of Velcro attachments.

8 Finally, pieces were brought to the site for assembly into the world's largest Mind Map.

The world's largest Mind Map – a staggering three storeys high and four storeys wide – with some of the 1,860 children who helped develop it, standing in the foreground in admiration of their own work

From the central image (the national flag of Singapore), the seven basic ordering ideas are (from '2 o'clock'): 'Nation' (brown branches), 'Origin' (blue branches), 'Lifestyle' (green branches), 'Industries' (purple branches), 'People' (red branches), Aspirations (blue branches) and Achievements' (yellow branches). K.C. Lee, CEO of the Singapore Institute of Management, one of the main sponsors of the event said:

> We are very happy to be a part of the creation of the world's largest Mind Map. Singapore's success is testimony to the power of harnessing intellectual capital. In today's global economy, intellectual capital is undeniably the most critical element in a country's success, and life-long learning, the new reality for any individual.
>
> The Mind Map depicts Singapore's history, pays tribute to Singapore's success and to the powers and wonders of the mind. It reminds us that even with limited material resources, through purely harnessing brain power, great things can be achieved.

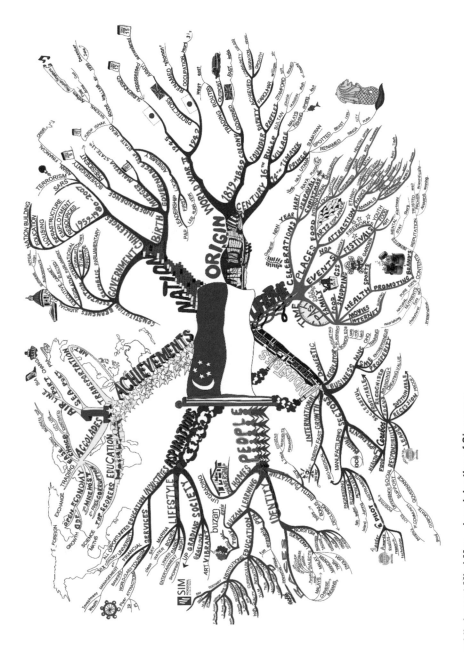

The world's largest Mind Map – in celebration of Singapore

Radiant thinking – radiant future

In order to examine the possibilities, it is necessary to return from the cosmos to the cortex, and to search for Rader Platt's beacons of hope in the welter of discouraging news about economics, pollution and the general global state. If we are to achieve a complete understanding of our current situation, and a more realistic interpretation of our future, it is necessary to look very closely at the single factor which most dramatically affects all future possibilities. This crucial factor is not the general environment, nor is it the theories of economics or psychology, nor even the 'basic aggressiveness of mankind', nor the 'irreversible tide of history'. The main, almost blindingly obvious factor is that which has been the subject of The Mind Map Book, and which in large part records, controls and directs the rest of the equation: the Radiant Thinking human brain.

In our increasing understanding of this incredibly complex and mysterious organ, in our increasing understanding of the family of mankind – ourselves and our radiant fellow humans – and in our increasing understanding of the inter-connectedness and relativity of all things, lies our hope for the future.

It can be so.

So be it!

Appendix

 At **www.imindmap.com** you will discover the official mind mapping software website, in which Tony Buzan's world famous and original Mind Maps® now in Version 4.0 are replicated and expanded. This is the closest a desktop or laptop computer or even an iPhone or other PDA can come to reflecting the imagination and association processes of true mind mapping carried out so effortlessly by that other ultimate computer, the human brain. **www.imindmap.com** includes:

Videos

Articles

Tutorials

Mind mapping tips

iMindmap templates

How to guides

buzan Welcome to Tony Buzan's world. Tony Buzan is the inventor of Mind Maps – the most powerful 'thinking tool' of our times. Discover more about Tony himself, and the transformative powers of mind mapping, memory and speed reading at **www.buzanworld.com**.

Tony Buzan's 'Festival of The Mind' online resources

The Festival of the Mind is a showcase event for the five learning 'mind sports' of memory, speed reading, IQ, creativity and mind mapping.

The first festival was held at the Royal Albert Hall in London in 1995 and was organised by Tony Buzan and Raymond Keene OBE. Since then, the festival has been held in the UK, alongside the World Memory Championships in Oxford, and in other countries around the world including Malaysia, China and Bahrain. The interest from the public in all five learning mind sports is growing worldwide so, not surprisingly, the festival is a big attraction. In fact, an event devoted solely to Mind Maps with Tony Buzan filled the Albert Hall again in 2006.

Each of the mind sports has its own council to promote, administer and recognise achievement in its field.

The World Memory Sports Council

The World Memory Sports Council is the independent governing body of the mind sport of memory and regulates competitions worldwide. Tony Buzan is the President of Council. You can visit the site at **www.worldmemorysportscouncil.com**.

The World Speed Reading Council was established to promote, train and recognise achievements in the field of speed reading worldwide. Apart from developing the ability to gain an understanding of large quantities of text in a short time, speed reading is one of the five learning 'mind sports' which can be practised competitively. The website is **www.worldspeedreadingcouncil.com**.

Appendix

Mind Mapping ® is a 'Thought Organisation Technique' invented by the international author and expert on the brain, Tony Buzan, in 1971. The World Mind Mapping Council administers and promotes the sport and also awards the prestigious title of Mind Mapping World Champion. The current reigning World Champion is Phil Chambers. Visit the site at **www.worldmindmappingcouncil.com**.

Creativity is defined by E. Paul Torrance, the doyen of creativity testing, as follows: 'Creativity is a process of becoming sensitive to problems, deficiencies, gaps in knowledge, missing elements, disharmonies and so on; identifying the difficulty; searching for solutions; making guesses or formulating hypotheses about the deficiencies; testing and re-testing these hypotheses and possibly modifying and retesting them; and finally communicating the results.' Creativity is one of the five learning mind sports along with mind mapping, speed reading, IQ and memory. All of these skills positively impact on the others, and together they can help any individual to be more effective in whatever they choose to do. All five learning mind sports are featured in the Festival of the Mind. Visit **www.worldcreativitycouncil.com**.

Intelligence Quotient (IQ) is one of the five learning mind sports which include Mind Mapping, Creativity, Speed Reading and Memory.

The World IQ Council can be contacted at **www.worldiqcouncil.com** and you can test your IQ on this site as well.

The Worldwide Brain Club, set up by the Buzan Organisation, encourages the formation of brain clubs worldwide. These have flourished for many years and bring together mind mapping, creativity, IQ, speed reading and memory. Practising each of these disciplines positively impacts on the others. Using Mind Maps, for example, helps with creativity as it presents ideas in a brain friendly way that inspires new ideas. Working on memory techniques makes the brain more capable in every other area in the same way that working out in a gym build muscles.

Brain Clubs, whether set up in a school or college, or within an organisation or company, create a supportive environment where all its members share the same objective, to give their personal 'neck top computer' the best operating system possible. Buzan Centres Worldwide provide qualified trainers in all of these areas. See **www.buzanworld.com** and **www.worldbrainclub.com**.

The Brain Trust is a registered charity which was founded in 1990 by Tony Buzan with one objective: to maximise the ability of each and every individual to unlock and deploy the vast capacity of their brain. Its charter includes promoting research into study of thought processes, the investigation of the mechanics of thinking, manifested in learning, understanding, communication, problem-solving, creativity and decision-making. In 2008 Professor (Baroness) Susan Greenfield won its 'Brain of the Century' award. Visit **www.braintrust.org.uk**.

The International Academy of Mental World Records, at **www.mentalworldrecords.com**, exists to recognise the achievements of Mental Athletes around the world. In addition to arbiting world record attempts and awarding certificates of achievement, the Academy is also linked to the International Festival of the Mind, which showcases mental achievements in the five learning mind sports of memory, speed reading, creativity, mind mapping and IQ.

Online resources

www.buzanworld.com

www.imindmap.com

www.worldmemorychampionships.com

www.worldmindmappingcouncil.com

www.schoolsmemorychampionships.com

www.braintrust.org.uk

www.festivalofthemind.com

www.worldcreativitycouncil.com

www.mentalworldrecords.com

www.worldbrainclub.com

www.worldspeedreadingcouncil.com

www.worldiqcouncil.com

www.buzanworld.com/lm_Tony_Buzan.htm

Index

and learning 9–10
memorising with Mind Maps 89
Mind Maps for 85, 87–91
  cluster data 88
  memorising 89
  relaxed concentration 88
  repeat data 88
mnemonic function of notes 110
and pictures 46
reviewing Mind Maps 69
and speed Mind Maps 70–1
and visual association exercises 49,
  51–2
memory trace 7
mental blocks 55
mental literacy 13, 196–200
mental maps, forming 7
'messy' Mind Map 73-5
metabolic pathways 24–5
Microsoft Outlook 179
Microsoft Project 182
Mind Maps 3
  birth of 10
  characteristics 31–2
  defining 31–4
  four danger areas 70–5
  full 56–7
  mirroring Radiant Thinking 25–6
  operations manual 58–75
  top 10 Mind Mapping tips 67–8
  see also branches (Mind Maps)
mini Mind Map exercises
  happiness 37–9, 41, 48
    extended 52
  images 48–9
mirroring Radiant Thinking 25–6
'missing' memories 89–90
mnemonic function of notes 110
mobile phone technology 189
monthly Mind Map diaries 133, 134
movement of images 62
MRP (Material Requirements Planning)
  189
Muhammad Ali 12
multidimensional thinking 25, 29
multilateral thinking 12–13
multiple-mind Mind Maps 151–2, 153
multipolar neurons 6

Naiman, Katarina 141
Naisbitt, John, *Megatrends 2000* 144–5

nature's Mind Map 34
negative emotional reactions 75
negative phrases, dangers of 72–3
negotiations, and computer Mind Maps
  184–5
neuronal pathways 7
neurons 5, 6, 8
Nickerson, R.S. 45–6
non Mind Maps 70, 71
note-making/taking
  functions of notes 109–11
  and geniuses 13–15
  and global 'sleeping sickness' 19–20
  Mind Maps for note taking 109–15
    from books 111–12
    from lectures 112–14
    overcoming obstacles 114
  results of research on 20–1
  styles 17–19
  see also linear notes
novels, revising 112
number-weighting decisions 101

O'Brien, Dominic 192
observation skills 80
observing images 61
oral tradition and memory 87
organic Mind Map lines 66

paper for Mind Maps
  artistic 77
  size and position of 67
parabrains, and decision-making 102
paradigm shifts 96–7
past goals, and self-analysis 122
pattern-recognition 11
PDAs (Personal Digital Assistants), and
  images 46–8
pens 67
performance appraisals, and computer
  Mind Maps 187, 188
personal goal setting, and computer
  Mind Maps 185
personal problem-solving, Mind Maps
  for 125–6
phrases, development of phrase
  statements 72–3, 74
pictures 67
  drawing 46
  and lecture notes 113
  thinking and communicating in 44–5